Discovery

Jensen Glennon-Dodd

Discovery

Vanguard Press

Vanguard Press is an imprint of
Pegasus Elliot Mackenzie Publishers Ltd.
www.pegasuspublishers.com

First Published in 2024

Vanguard Press
Sheraton House Castle Park
Cambridge England

Printed & Bound in Great Britain

Dedication

This book is dedicated to Granny who always has a wise word and my mother whose glass is always half full.

Preface

Have you ever had a brief explanation of vitamins and minerals from advertisements?

Advertisements, from television adverts to magazines or even social media posts showcasing how the latest trend of celebrities take this special Vitamin or magical mineral every morning to turn back the clock and feel twenty years younger? Or even better, look twenty years younger. If this sounds completely alien to you, not to worry as we are going to Discover all of this throughout our journey together.

While having breakfast, have you ever looked on the back of your cereal box (Corn Flakes are my favourite) and see it stating in bold **Vitamin B6** 1.2 MG and thought what on Earth does that mean, but hey at least it says Vitamin on it so it must be good, right? …

And guess what? You would be right, that Vitamins are good for us, in fact Vitamins play a vital role in our overall health and wellness, and without them, well let's just say that you would certainly be a duller version of yourself, flat looking skin, lower mood, a poor metabolism, lower energy and having trouble fighting illness, isn't this a wonderful way to start our Discovery?

Despite millions of people having a basic understanding of the importance of vitamins and minerals, unfortunately too many people lack a wider understanding of how they benefit us on a daily basis and enable us to feel our best. What if I asked you what the difference is between fat soluble vitamins and water-soluble vitamins? Could you tell me? What if I asked you which two essential minerals compete with one another in the body and an imbalance can be a detriment to our health?

That's when this book comes in handy, be prepared to come on a discovery with me where we will explore the essential vitamins and minerals. By the end of this book, you will have a much deeper understanding of the different functions of vitamins and minerals and how they impact our everyday lives, including food sources, even if you're a vegan or vegetarian. After always having a keen interest and doing lots of research, I felt that there was a lack of an accessible book to everyone from different ages and circumstances that gives a basic complete overview for everyone of different ages and circumstances, so this is where I come in, I just decided to write one myself, whether you just want a quick reference or wanting a stepping stone to deepen your knowledge, I believe that this book can help you.

I hope that you find this book as useful as I have, I wanted to spread the message that anyone of any background can look after their health, I really do believe that your health is true wealth, more valuable than any amount of money. Good health without any doubt can extend a seventy-year-old lifespan to a ninety-year-old lifespan. You get another twenty years watching your grandkids grow up, or spending time with closest friends, not sure about you, but it sounds worth it to me.

While I am not saying that having adequate amounts of every vitamin is going to make you invulnerable to every age related ailment, what I am saying however, is that it can greatly reduce the chances of becoming seriously ill as you age, what if I said that some vitamins contribute to supporting our immune system, what if I told you that another mineral is vital in transporting oxygen around in our bodies, what if I told you that one mineral can greatly help support male fertility. Feeling interested now?

Remember those old Nerf adverts that used to be on TV with the motto "Its nerf or nothing?" Well, how about "Its health or nothing" You can have all the riches in the world, but how can you enjoy it if you don't have the health too?

Good health means, playing with your grandchildren, going on a night out with your closest friends, going travelling wherever you want, no health no fun, no health no life. Living with poor health appears to have a huge detriment to how much we can enjoy life? Your alive but you're not living! It doesn't sound like fun going to the Doctors back and forth.

I know that this may be tough to listen to, but I am trying to be realistic with you, it can be an unfortunate reality that some people do live with daily.

Having a wider knowledge of what makes us healthy and putting that knowledge into practice can certainly put the probabilities in your favour of living a happier and longer life. Now that sounds more positive and worthwhile.

No matter how old you are, eighteen or eighty, I firmly believe that anyone has the potential to make a small positive step to greater health, by having a greater awareness of how our body functions, also how we fuel it. Nevertheless, it is always better to start sooner rather than later and that day starts TODAY! Not tomorrow or next week or next month or next year. TODAY!

TODAY is the only guarantee that we have.

You could even print that word out and stick it on the wall as a daily reminder for yourself, ready let's shift our Discovery into 1st gear and let's get rolling.

Are you ready to move on with our Discovery together? I certainly am.

Before we start on our journey together, I just want to clarify that this book can be split up into three separate sections; in the first section we are going to Discover each Vitamin including their individual benefits, in the second section we are going to Discover more about what the most important minerals do, and finally in our third and last section we are going to Discover several lesser known benefits of the most known Herbal Remedies. What you are going to learn is just an overall core knowledge of the Vitamins, Minerals and Herbal Remedies I think that if I went into detail about each Vitamin and mineral you might feel overwhelmed and lose interest, so I have tried to condense and give you a solid foundation that you will be able to build on. I must also admit that I certainly don't know everything, despite learning a great deal about Vitamins and health, I do still have a lot to learn on my own journey as well.

Before we begin, I just want to clarify the differences between Fat Soluble Vitamins and Water-Soluble Vitamins as I will be referring to these phrases a lot throughout the Vitamins section of this book, I want you to 100 per cent know what I'm talking about. Fat soluble Vitamins (Vitamin A, D, E, K) are stored in the liver until they are needed (many are stored for longer than five months) as they are stored in the liver it is more difficult to be deficient in these Vitamins, however, because of this there is the danger of excessive levels building up in the body causing Toxicity and a Fatty Liver (so make sure to watch how much you're taking, particularly as a supplement) A good way to remember the Fat Soluble Vitamins is the Acronym DALEK (**exterminate**!) with the L standing for Liver, where the Fat Soluble Vitamins are stored.

On the other hand, Water Soluble Vitamins (Vitamin B, C) are not stored in the Liver, but rather when they enter the bloodstream are absorbed into the body's tissues straight away. Unlike, the Fat-Soluble Vitamins our bodies remove the Water Soluble Vitamins from our body once our bodies have had enough of them, and are removed via our urine, therefore its vital that we get these Vitamins in our daily diet, the Water Soluble Vitamins are also easier to be deficient in due to our daily need for them, but also much more difficult to overdose on.

Vitamin A (The Protection Vitamin)

We begin together with the first Vitamin we are going to discover, it is also known as *the protection Vitamin*. Vitamin A is probably best associated with protecting our eye health and reducing the rate of macular degeneration as we age, essentially Vitamin A helps to preserve our eyesight for longer. Not only this, but Vitamin A also prevents night blindness (so there is really some truth in the saying that carrots help you see in the dark) Vitamin A helps to support our eyes by helping to support the health of our retina, one of the key roles of the retina is to help catch light that passes through the lens of our eye and helps to convert it into the world that we see around us, not only this but Vitamin A is also important in helping to support the Cornea, which is the outer layer of the eye, the Cornea is extremely important in allowing us to be able to focus on near or longer distance objects. So, just remember Vitamin A is the key to allowing you to not have to wear glasses by helping our eyes to convert light into chemical signals. Vitamin A is also important for helping to support eye development in newly born babies, but also Vitamin A can help your baby's development in other ways, such as supporting the immune system (which we will learn later) this as a result can help to reduce the chances of a newly born baby catching an infectious disease and becoming ill (super baby power!)

Vitamin A also keeps the immune system strong in adults as well, helping to stop those germs and viruses in their tracks and causing illness. To be more specific, Vitamin A supports the production of the powerful force packing white blood cells, which help trap and kill bad bacteria and other pathogens (bacteria that can cause illness) from your blood stream. Therefore, if you are deficient in Vitamin A (which is quite rare to be fair) then you are at a higher risk of catching infections and will inevitably have a longer recovery time if it's your luck to catch an infection or cold, as Vitamin A is crucial in helping to stimulate the body's production of White blood cells, also Vitamin A is important in keeping the White Blood Cells strong and sturdy when they need to fight against those Pathogens.

It has also been suggested that Vitamin A can also support the skin and even reduce acne (good news for teenagers) although it is not fully known why. One possible explanation for this is that Retinol, which is found naturally in Vitamin A may improve skin elasticity and helping to prevent sagging wrinkly skin by helping remove damaged elastin fibres but by also promoting the formation of new blood vessels therefore helping to remove all of the dirt, oil and dead skin cells from the surface of the skin. Vitamin A is also important in helping to maintain a healthy dermis and epidermis, don't fear these names, they are just the names for the upper layers of the skin, especially when Vitamin A is applied topically.

Another important thing to know is that Vitamin A actually comes in two forms, Beta Carotene and Retinol (yes that Retinol in the fancy skincare adverts on TV) Retinol comes from animal foods such as Liver, and is easily stored in the body so could potentially cause Toxic effects, however remember only if in high doses, if you ate ten livers then I would be concerned, so there's no need to worry too much. Retinol can also be applied topically on the face, and is well known to be a powerful anti-aging secret among Dermatologists, this is because Retinol can help support cell turnover (the formation of new cells onto the surface of the skin) as a result helping to keep our skin firmer and prevent skin dullness, if you're using Retinol as a facial moisturiser then it thankfully won't carry the same side effects compared to if its consumed. The second form and perhaps less interesting is Beta Carotene, which comes from vegetables such as carrots, and is converted by the body to use rather than stored, therefore Beta Carotene as a whole doesn't carry the same risks as Retinol but remember applying Retinol externally carries no side effects. Only when it is consumed.

Potential Risks

While having too much Vitamin A is usually rare, there are still some potential risks to keep your eyes open for (like what I did there?). The main risk associated with

Vitamin A is that too much Vitamin A over the longer term may cause slight Toxicity which can result in rashes and abdominal pain.

Vitamin A over dosage can also lead to an increased risk of fractures in older people, by weakening bones, hence increasing the risk of Osteoporosis. Would you like to maybe Discover what decrease the amount of Vitamin A in the body? I would! Things that can deplete Vitamin A tend to be eating too much Junk food as well as consuming too much Caffeine (Coffee and Tea) can all deplete levels of Vitamin A in the body.

Also, anyone who is Pregnant or is thinking about having a baby should also be careful of taking Vitamin A, especially if taking it as a supplement, as too much may harm an unborn Baby, therefore certainly stay away from Liver products. (Sorry to those who like Liver)

However, despite these risks, don't be fearful, as overdosing on Vitamin A is rare, if you stick to a balanced diet and don't go crazy on the Liver.

Food Sources

Vitamin A can be found in a wide variety of foods that we eat daily that you probably wouldn't have even realised.

These foods include Apples, Avocados (Good source of Vitamin E as well) Butter, Carrots, Cheese, Cod Liver Oil, Eggs (Particularly the Yolk) Milk, Nuts and Yogurts. So a lot of our Vitamin A intake can come from dairy sources, it might be more suitable in this case for Vegans in particular to take a Vitamin A supplement.

Summary

- Vitamin A is a Fat-Soluble Vitamin meaning that it is stored in the Liver, therefore remaining in the body for longer, compared to the water-soluble Vitamins, as a result they don't need to be consumed as much.

- Vitamin A overall supports eye health, helping to prevent Macular Degeneration as we age and helping to prevent night blindness.

- Vitamin A supports the immune system by supporting the production of White Blood Cells, that are crucial in protecting the body against infection and disease.

- Vitamin A supports overall health of the skin, by effectively supporting natural moisturising of the skin and supporting a healthy dermis and epidermis, these are the top two layers of the skin, especially when it is applied topically in the form of Retinol.

Vitamin B (The Energy Vitamin)

WOW! Did you feel that rapid acceleration! I have never felt so energetic and full of *ENERGY* in my life! Ahhh, the joys of Vitamin B. Are you one of those people who have the desire to do more, get out more, be more, live life a little more, but you're simply just too tired to be able to, and what doesn't help is the long and often exhausting working week. Its Work, Cook, Eat, Sleep Repeat. Well, you're in luck as with the help of Vitamin B you'll soon be making the most of every minute every of day. Time for what? I've constantly got fun plans after work. Now does that sound better.

As a rule (we will get onto the subcategories of Vitamin B later) Vitamin B is that Vitamin that really gives us that get up and go to really rock life, you'll soon be unstoppable. While the B vitamins do not supply energy directly to us, they help your body effectively use carbohydrates, fats, and proteins as fuel which will be transformed into energy in the mitochondria (the cell of chemical reactions which produces energy) in the cell through digestion and absorption. Vitamin B is also Water Soluble, meaning that it is not stored in the Liver, as a result the body disposes the B Vitamins once it's had enough of them, therefore it is essential that you consume every day from diet, or supplementation if necessary. The best news of all is because the B Vitamins are excreted in the Urine, even after a couple of hours, means that it is virtually impossible to consume too much and overdose, unlike the Fat-Soluble Vitamins, such as Vitamin D, so you don't need to look out for how much you're consuming.

Have you also ever had one of those days where you feel like the world is overwhelming you a little bit? Well, my friend, you're in luck as Vitamin B helps to balance emotional health while helping to keep stress to a minimum, this is because as a rule of thumb, the B Vitamins help in balancing out the neurotransmitters in the Brain. Fancy some evidence? Well to put your mind at ease (like what I did there) in 2014 research by Swinburne University in Australia concluded that there was a 20 per cent reduction in "work-related stress" in those consuming higher levels of B Vitamins. So, to remove the stress you know where to go.

Now let's look a little deeper into the specific twelve subcategories of the B Vitamins and discover their own unique individual benefits.

B1 (Thiamin) - Here we are, the first member of the B vitamin family. Probably the main function of Thiamin is to help turn the food that we consume into ENERGY! which allows us to keep on going when life gets a little overwhelming. Thiamin is also important in helping to keep our nervous system healthy, I'm sure that you have heard it been said before, it is true that the nervous system is crucial in allowing us to function well, its main two functions allowing us to simply move and breathe, but Thiamin is also important in allowing the electrical impulses to travel around our body more effectively, which simply just allows our nervous system to work. Just a little side note, your body is not able to produce thiamine for itself. However, no need to panic, as you can usually get all the Thiamin you need from diet. In rare cases, a deficiency may result in a condition called Beriberi, causing muscle and psychological weakness and even confusion.

However, one lesser-known function of Thiamin is that it can act as an effective insect repellent, no more fear of those dreaded insect bites. This is because Thiamin releases through the skin when we sweat, Thiamin has an odour that is thankfully undetectable to humans. (but something that those nasty insects certainly don't like) I wouldn't want to know what this odour smells like, would you? Thankfully now you can say farewell to being covered in inspect bites from an army of mosquitoes after just waking up, it would be a great way to start the morning.

Food sources of Thiamin include fortified Breakfast cereals, all types of meat, seeds (Chia seeds, sunflower seeds, soybeans) and Nuts like Almonds and cashews

B2 (Riboflavin) - Now what if I told you that you can say goodbye to having to worry about the opticians, about having to have stronger and stronger glasses, and constantly changing vision, but best of all, no worries about eye operations! Riboflavin can help all of that as it can help to preserve our eyesight as we age, this will be especially needed for you to point out the directions of which road I need to take to get to the right destination so we can have a successful Discovery together. It's believed that Riboflavin can support our eye health because of its ability to protect our eyes from Oxidative stress, which is one of the most common reasons for degenerating eye health, especially because as we age, our eye muscles naturally begin to weaken and we our more vulnerable to those unwanted eye conditions like Cataracts and Glaucoma. Riboflavin can also help to prevent night blindness, again this can be put down to Riboflavin protecting our eyes from Oxidative stress, so in this regard Riboflavin can be seen to share very similar properties with Vitamin A, now that's what I call some serious eye power! Furthermore, Riboflavin also helps to break down fats, proteins, and carbohydrates, and keeps a steady supply of energy flowing through your body. Having adequate amounts of Riboflavin are also important in supporting the absorption of Iron into the body, whereas on the contrary being deficient in Riboflavin may increase Iron loss in the body. It is also arguably more important for women, especially Women who are pregnant and who are going through the Menopause to get adequate amounts of Riboflavin compared to men, as Women have a greater need for Iron (We will learn about this in greater detail later on in the Iron section), and the effectiveness of Iron being absorbed into the body can be increased by having good amounts of Riboflavin.

However, one extremely common side effect of Riboflavin is that if it's taken as a supplement, it will probably cause your urine to turn bright yellow! but it is completely normal and harmless.

Food sources of Riboflavin include Blueberries, Breakfast cereals, Eggs, Milk, Nuts, Raspberries, fish (Salmon in particular) and Tomatoes (Powerful antioxidant there)

B3 (Niacin) - Like with all the other B vitamins, Niacin helps to break down fats and protein, converting the food we consume into energy, helping us to get through the long working week. However, one unique trait of Niacin is that it has the potential of supporting healthy cholesterol levels (good for those who like a bit fine dining) Niacin has been shown to help reduce LDL or 'bad' cholesterol and increase levels of HDL or 'good' cholesterol. Therefore, Niacin can help to reduce the chances of heart disease reducing the strain put on our Heart, remember that healthy Cholesterol and Niacin levels leads to a healthy and happy Heart. That's what I call a good combination.

Niacin helps to release chemicals (Prostaglandins) that help your blood vessels widen, and as a result improves blood flow and reduces the chances of developing high blood pressure, overall resulting in greater heart health.

One main potential side effect of Niacin is that it may cause flushing of the skin, this is because Niacin causes the small blood vessels in your skin to dilate so more blood can rush through. However, flushes will only be caused through high dose supplementation. Likewise, supplementing in the longer term with Niacin, may cause mild tingling, but this tends to happen in the longer term.

Like with the other B Vitamins, Niacin can be found in a variety of different food sources including Breakfast cereals, Eggs, meat, fish, and wheat flour.

B5 (Pantothenic Acid) – Ever wanted to experience what it was like to be Albert Einstein? Well congratulations as these are where the Pantothenic acids come into their own. It has been scientifically proven that Pantothenic supports learning, specifically on mental performance and sharpness (Good for anyone taking a test) One of the reasons that Pantothenic Acid can improve our brain health, is because of its importance in supporting the Nerve cells that are connected to the brain, but it's also believed that Pantothenic Acid can also protect these structures from Oxidative stress, which is a common reason for brain degenerative diseases such as Alzheimer's.

Pantothenic Acid also has the potential to reduce anxiety and chronic stress, perhaps because of its ability to improve mental performance and focus, to be more specific, Pantothenic acid reduces anxiety by helping to regulate the stress hormone Cortisol (the hormone that produces stress during fight or flight situations), while at the same time helping with the production of the hormone Serotonin, which is one of the main hormones that regulates mood and makes us HAPPY! Disclaimer Alert! Now while it is good to an extent to reduce Cortisol, there is no doubt that Cortisol is still beneficial to us in small amounts, it's a natural system built into us that regulates the "Fight or Flight" Mechanism in us. So having a little bit of Cortisol is a good thing, it helps to keep us in tip top shape.

So, to put it more simply Pantothenic acid is a powerful mood enhancer and brain booster that will allow you to complete complex math complications within seconds (I wish I could do that)

Pantothenic Acid can be found in various food sources including mushrooms, vegetables, eggs, fish, nuts, Wholegrains, meat, Avocados, sunflower seeds, Tomatoes

B6 (Pyridoxine)- Are you feeling that your hormones are a little bit out of control? An up and down rollercoaster mood? Tired, sleepy, drained? Trouble with digestion? Well, Pyridoxine can help with just that, especially for women whose hormones tend to be sensitive to aggravate, which can be more noticeable during menopause. This is because Pyridoxine helps to regulate the female hormones Oestrogen and Progesterone which are usually affected during the menopause, and mensuration, so Pyridoxine helps to support healthy aging and post menopause in women (yay) Menopause, what Menopause?

Do you ever feel like you're having a case of the blues? Well you are in luck! Pyridoxine can help to support our mood, this could be because Pyridoxine is important for creating neurotransmitters that help to regulate our emotions (no more blues, get in!) these specific hormones include serotonin and dopamine (but dopamine without all the drugs and of course the awaited Dopamine crash to come) but the other way that Pyridoxine may help with regulating mood is by decreasing high levels of the Amino acid called homocysteine (to use its fancy scientific name) which has been linked to increased depression and higher levels of anxiety, this is in part because higher levels of homocysteine has been linked to being deficient in certain Vitamins, most notably the B vitamins which are known to support brain function. Check this out, because Pyridoxine lowers homocysteine, there is a potential to lower the risk of Alzheimer's (which is fantastic, what great news)

Overall, you should not experience any side effects from Pyridoxine, as it would be nearly impossible to consume excessive amounts from diet alone. However, taking more than 1000 MG from a supplement (unless recommended by a doctor) may cause nerve damage and numbness in the longer term.

Foods sources for Pyridoxine include your typical breakfast cereals, pork, oats, dairy, bananas (yum yum) and peanuts.

Just a small side note that the Friendly Bacteria that naturally live in your bowel can also produce Pyridoxine, so keeping your Bowel and Gut happy may also result in greater Pyridoxine levels. However, on the flip side, higher levels of bad bacteria may inhibit the body's ability to produce Pyridoxine.

B7 (Biotin) – Ever looked in the mirror and wished that you were blessed with beautiful hair like Rapunzel? Well, you're at the right place then, as Biotin can help to make that wish come true.

Firstly, Biotin has the potential to help the strength of hair and nails, but there is also some evidence which suggests that Biotin may also help with improving symptoms such as brittle nails, balding or scaly rashes, which tend to show in people who are deficient in Biotin. Biotin has the potential to help support hair growth by helping to turn the food that we eat into energy (Like with all the other B Vitamins), but this energy can be used by the body to trigger the production of the protein Keratin instead, which is important in determining the speed that our hair and nails grow. The more keratin production the faster these will grow. Another positive benefit of Biotin is that it can help those who are wanting a better tan for the summer, this is because as we learnt Biotin can help with the production of Keratin, but Keratin is also important in helping the production of Melanin, which is the pigment found in the skin that turns the skin brown after exposure to sunlight (We will explore more of this in the Copper section)

Biotin is also needed by the body in very small amounts to help the body metabolise carbohydrates and Amino acids which in turn then breaks down fatty acids (don't worry not all acids are evil) and glucose.

Overall, Biotin doesn't carry any particularly alarming side effects as like with all of the other B Vitamins, however, in higher doses Acne may be caused as Biotin increases sebum production in the body, which can make the skin Oily, making the skin more prone to spots and ruptures, so it wouldn't hurt to maybe keep a nice facial cleanser nearby.

Food sources of Biotin include almonds, whole grains, eggs, sardines, pecans, dried fruits, cucumber, oats, strawberries, cauliflower, milk

B9 (Folic Acid) – Trying for a baby or currently going through a pregnancy, but you're feeling the burn? Well guess what? Folic Acid is here to help.

Before we start I just to want to clarify that there are two types of B9, Folic acid is a synthetic type of vitamin B9. It is used in vitamin supplements and added to certain fortified foods such as cereals and our bodies can use this form more efficiently than folates.

The other type of B9 is Folate which is a natural type of vitamin B9. It's found in green, leafy vegetables, some meats, citrus fruits, legumes, brown rice, and wholemeal bread. Folate (more than Folic Acid) helps to protect us against the development of Cancer by helping to protect our DNA, Cancer is caused when our DNA acts abnormally causing uncontrolled cell growth, which is when we see tumours develop on people.

If you're planning for pregnancy, it's recommended that you take folic acid supplements before you conceive and until you're at least twelve weeks pregnant.

Folic Acid works hard to support the rapid cell growth that happens during the early development of tissues and organs during conception and in the first few weeks of pregnancy. As a result of this, Folic Acid can help to reduce the chances your baby being born with defects.

Furthermore, having good levels of Folic acid can also improve Egg quality and growth, therefore as a result increasing the chances of having a successful pregnancy.

Folic acid can also be beneficial to men, this is because some studies suggest that there could be a link between the amount of folic acid in a man's diet and the genetic quality of his sperm. It has also been suggested that Folic acid can keep blood vessels open and clear of blockages, which could benefit males at a higher risk of cardiovascular disease

Reported side effects of too much Folic acid include Feeling sick (for pregnant women this is more likely to be morning sickness) and bloating or wind. Consuming excessive amounts of Folic Acid can ironically cause opposite beneficial effects on pregnancy, as excessive

Folic Acid can unfortunately increase the chances of gene mutation, which can increase the chances of the baby having disabilities.

Good food sources for Folic acid/Folates include Spinach, broccoli, pork, Oranges, and everyone's favourite, delicious Brussels sprouts!

B10 (PABA) – Here we are, another brilliant beauty Vitamin, (sometimes I think it's called PAPA, rather than PABA) In many ways Paba has very similar properties to Biotin in that it supports our hair. However, there are slight differences. Just as a side note, PABA is not strictly regarded as a vitamin on its own, but its activity closely resembles the other B Vitamins. It is typically found in B complex supplements.

Firstly, PABA may help to support the natural colour of our hair and skin, this is in part because it is also thought that PABA can provide a protective effect against the damage that is caused by the UV rays from the sun that can cause damage to our skin and hair.

Another benefit of PABA is that it also has the potential of helping the production of its close ally, Folate, and in supplements PABA is usually contained within Folic acid.

However, research into PABA has overall been mixed, with some studies showing that people have unfortunately had allergic reactions to sunscreens containing PABA, causing red, itchy rashes (so seems a bit counterintuitive if it is meant to protect you) and also taking high doses of PABA supplements is not considered safe for those with liver and kidney issues, so always check with a doctor just in case. If you're using a cosmetic product that contains PABA and you notice a rash or skin irritation, best to discontinue its use. So be sure to keep your eyes open just in case any rashes pop up.

Food sources of PABA include wholegrain products and organic meats

B12 - (Cobalamin)

NOW! This is what I really call the power packing B vitamin, once you learn about this, you'll be dancing on the ceiling in no time!

Cobalamin is probably regarded as the most important member of the B Vitamin family and is probably the most popular and well-known as well. Cobalamin plays a vital role in allowing our body to convert the foods that we eat into ENERGY! This is partially because Cobalamin is very important in helping the body to produce red blood cells (They carry Oxygen round the body from the Lungs, so very important indeed!) and also helping to make DNA, because of this Cobalamin may help to reduce the chances of developing cancer, as one of the causes of Cancer is if our DNA becomes damaged from Oxidative stress, this makes Cobalamin extremely important in our growth and allowing our cells to reproduce, if our bodies were unable to produce DNA, well let's just say that we would be in a little bit of a bit of a sticky situation at the moment. Going quickly back to red blood cells, Cobalamin is important in not only producing red blood cells, but also keeping them strong and healthy, to distinguish a healthy blood cell to a poorer one, healthy blood cells tend to be smaller in size and a nice round shape like an orange, but in the case of a deficiency in Cobalamin, not only will there be a shortage of red blood cells in the body, but because of the red blood cell shortage, the red blood cells that do remain tend to be larger in order to compensate for the lesser numbers, but the problem of this is that there will be more strain put on the blood vessels, and then of course more strain put onto the Heart.

Cobalamin also has the potential of making you HAPPY! Yippee! Like with Pyridoxine (B6) Cobalamin has the potential of increasing Serotonin production in the body, making you feel like you're a little more on top of the world (I wish I felt like that a little more often).

Cobalamin is also essential for the proper functioning and development of the brain and nerve cells. It plays an important role in the maintenance of the sheaths that cover and protect the nerves of the central and peripheral nervous system (the transmission of nerve signals between the spinal cord to different parts of the body), ensuring a fast and effective nerve impulse transmission, so having good amounts of Cobalamin can help to reduce dementia (meaning a super sharp brain, complex math calculations? No Problem!). So, a good sign of potentially being deficient in Cobalamin is feeling a little sluggish. As a result, Cobalamin acts as an effective protector of the nervous system and without an effective nervous system, there is an increased risk of stress and anxiety, as Cobalamin helps to regulate the amount of Cortisol that the Adrenal glands produce, which Cobalamin helps to prevent (always a bonus) so Cobalamin can help bring you back down to Earth if you're feeling a little on edge.

What makes Cobalamin so popular is that because of its dietary sources, making it accessible to a wide variety of people, although those who are vegetarian and vegan may find it more difficult to consume Cobalamin from diet alone, and that's when supplementation tends to become quite popular. In general, older people tend to be prone to Cobalamin deficiency, therefore a higher risk of mental impairment and brain fog. So, if you're getting on a bit or Vegan, it wouldn't hurt to consider taking a Cobalamin supplement every day.

One main benefit of also taking Cobalamin is that the risks of any side effects are minimum (probably the least common of any of the B Vitamin family) hence a reason for its popularity.

Food sources for Cobalamin include Breakfast cereals, bread, Beef, Dairy products, Eggs, all types of fish (Cod, Salmon, Herring, Tuna and even sardines) and nutritional yeast

Summary

-    Overall Vitamin B plays a crucial role in our health by helping release energy from the food we eat, effectively nourishing our bodies, helping us to keep going when a brick wall hits (That must hurt)

- The B Vitamins are also important in supporting normal brain function by keeping are neurons in tip top shape which has the effect of greater memory skills and attention.

- As Vitamin B is a water-soluble Vitamin, it is important that we have a daily intake of this Vitamin as its excreted daily through the Urine. However, Vitamin B is highly accessible through a wide variety of foods such as whole grains.

- Vitamin B has been linked to helping remove harmful substances from the body which can lead to an increased risk of heart disease and stroke.

Vitamin C (The Healing Vitamin)

Are you one of those people who puts in every precaution when winter comes to avoid getting sick? However, after everything, Guess what? You still get ill and think, WHAT! I did everything, how am I ill? I work out, my diet is brilliant, I wore my winter coat, I kept myself warm, I took all the necessary precautions, I'm only twenty years old. Still bewildered how you're still ill, despite everything you've done? It's just cold after cold after cold.

Well no worries friend, as Vitamin C could be the answer to your problems, say goodbye to those terrible colds during those gloomy winter months when colds seem to be more widespread, but another great benefit is that Vitamin C can also improve the chances of having a quicker recovery time, so if you do get sick, instead of having to spend a couple of weeks in bed you will only have to put up with a weeks' worth of bed rest instead. If this sounds appealing then let's dive a little deeper shall we?

Probably the largest use for Vitamin C is to help with our immunity, particularly during the winter when those nasty germs are more prevalent. Vitamin C successfully boosts our immunity by encouraging the production of protective White blood cells such as phagocytes, that help to protect the body by destroying pathogens such as Viruses and Bacteria via the process of Phagocytosis.

Another way that Vitamin C boosts immunity is by improving the overall health of our White blood cells, because when the White blood cells are healthier, they are not as susceptible to damage from free radicals and are better equipped to fight off those unwanted Pathogens.

Vitamin C also has the potential of improving our overall skin health, so if you're ever looking in the mirror and wishing for better skin, then you're in luck. This is because Vitamin C has the potential of boosting collagen production in the body, Collagen is the protein that keeps skin elastic and beautifully young, but sadly declines with age. Now what's even better is because Vitamin C helps to keep collagen levels topped up, the rate of skin aging will be slowed (Just think anti-aging) Additionally Vitamin C supports our skin health due to its powerful antioxidant effects, helping us to fight back against the nasty free radicals that can cause damage to your good looks, free radicals are cells from the external environment that can cause damage to our own cells most notably from pollution and smoking, that speeds up aging. The protection that Vitamin C provides us, helps combat against Oxidative stress, can also protect us against mental damage such as Alzheimer's, as Oxidative stress also has the potential of causing inflammation near the brain and nerves (Just think two in one, beauty and mind protection:)

Have you ever been ripping it at the gym, felt good about yourself but afterwards been really struggling with soreness and stiffness. Well, guess what? Vitamin C can help with post exercise soreness and recovery too, so no more suffering after your workout. Like with supporting immunity, Vitamin C helps with soreness due to its anti-oxidant effects, when we exercise free radicals are produced such as Lactic Acid, which results in us becoming tired and sore, especially during Anaerobic Exercise, which is just a fancy name for short high intensity exercise, but excessive levels of Free Radicals can result in damage to the body such as injury to the joints however, Vitamin C can reduce the extent that free radicals damage the body and therefore provide us with more protection and reassurance that our bodies will be better able to cope with the stresses that we put it through.

Potential Risks

Vitamin C is a water-soluble Vitamin, meaning that it is not stored in the liver and is secreted by the Kidneys, so it is important that you consume an adequate amount of Vitamin C daily, therefore it is definitely harder to overdose, some side effects to take note on is the possibility of diarrhoea, nausea and abdominal cramps, these side effects however, tend come from supplementing on Vitamin C, rather than getting it from food sources. Even at high doses, vitamin C is not known to be toxic or to cause any serious adverse effects, so you should be A-OK :)

Just one last thing to also point out before I forget is careful with caffeine (sorry coffee and tea lovers) as it's known that Caffeine reduces the effectiveness of how Vitamin C is absorbed by the body. This is because Caffeine increases blood flow in the body, and as a result leads to more urinating, however, the Vitamin C is often removed from the body with the urine before the body has had a proper chance to absorb it.

The best sources of Vitamin C are most notably Citrus fruits, especially a nice big juicy ORANGE! For those who are a little sensitive to Citrus fruits, other good sources of Vitamin C include Broccoli, Blackcurrants, Cauliflower, Peppers (Spicy!) Potatoes and Kale

Summary

-    One of the biggest benefits of Vitamin C is that it helps increase our immunity, due to supporting the production of white blood cells that fight pathogens which can cause serious harm to the body
-    Vitamin C has protective effects on our skin by helping to increase the collagen levels in our body, this has the result of keeping the skin elastic and plump, and helps to protect against free radicals that speed up aging such as pollution

-   Vitamin C can also help soreness post exercise due to its antioxidant effects that help fight free radicals that build up during exercise therefore helping to decrease recovery time and preventing longer term injuries.

Vitamin D (The Sunshine Vitamin)

Have you ever pictured yourself sunbathing on an isolated Caribbean beach drinking a nice fresh Pina colada? No troubles, no worries, and most importantly full of happiness, relaxing at the beach? What is this brilliant mysterious Vitamin you might be asking yourself? What if I also told you that around half of Americans are deficient in this essential Vitamin. OK I bet your interested now!

Vitamin D out of all the Vitamins is arguably the most important Vitamin, partly because of how difficult it can be to get adequate amounts of Vitamin D from diet alone, as well as from the Sun, which can also be a difficult to get if you live in a more northern country. Before we get into the joys that Vitamin D can bring to you, let me tell you that Vitamin D is a Fat-Soluble Vitamin, well its actually more of a hormone than a Vitamin, meaning that it is stored in the Liver, so we do have to be careful not to get too much. Vitamin D also comes in two forms called D2 and D3. Vitamin D2 comes typically from mushrooms and is the form used in foods, such as fortified breakfast cereal (I must admit Corn Flakes are my favourite) On the other hand, Vitamin D3, which is also the best absorbed form of Vitamin D comes from the sun and is the biologically active form of the Vitamin, the Vitamin D that comes from the sun technically isn't D3, but the body magically converts it to D3 when it is absorbed into the Skin from the Sun, so don't be afraid to get a little bit of Sun exposure. The good news though is that both D2 and D3 forms can both be found in supplements that you can buy. However, if a person was extremely deficient in Vitamin D (more on that later) I would recommend taking D3 as a supplement, but to be fair most supplements nowadays are in the form of D3.

Now that's been said, shall we get into the wonders that Vitamin D can bring to you?

Overall, Vitamin D plays many Vital roles in the body and is even arguably the most important Vitamin. The first main benefit is that Vitamin D is extremely important in helping to boost our mood and helping to remove those blue feelings that we can get, especially in the cold winter months when there typically tends to be a lack of Sun, its partly why the January Blues are a thing, and why we tend to feel happier in the hot Sun, its Vitamin D! So, if you're feeling down and a bit fed up, it could be a Vitamin D deficiency, particularly if it's often. One possible explanation for how Vitamin D can help to boost our mood is by regulating Enzymes that are responsible for chemical reactions in the body, and the Enzyme reactions help to convert Tryptophan into serotonin, and Serotonin is extremely important in helping to regulate mood and reducing feelings of depression.

Another key function of Vitamin D is if you want to impress the Dentist and the Doctor, as Vitamin D can also help to support healthy bones and teeth (Say Goodbye to expensive Dentist bills) Vitamin D helps to support our teeth health because Vitamin D possesses some powerful anti-oxidant properties, as a result this reduces the risk of tooth decay and nasty gum disease, all detrimental factors to our dental health. Another way that Vitamin D can support our dental health is because of how Vitamin D effectively utilises Calcium in the body, did you know that Calcium, along with phosphorus, makes up the raw material that makes up our tooth structure and enamel, but Calcium can't be effectively used by the body if we don't have adequate amounts of Vitamin D. The importance of Vitamin D in helping to absorb Calcium into the body also plays an important role in helping to ensure that our bones stay strong and healthy, especially as we age when we start to lose bone density, if we lack both Vitamin D and Calcium this can over an extended period of time lead to a condition called Osteoporosis, in which the bones become more fragile and will eventually lose density making them more susceptible to breaks. Therefore Vitamin D helps to support our overall bone density and keep them nice and strong as we age preventing other degenerative conditions such as Osteoporosis that increases the risk of breaks and fractures. So, a Vitamin D a day helps to keeps the Doctor and hospital away.

Vitamin D is probably the only Vitamin that the Government (and don't forget me of course) would actually recommend taking daily as a supplement as its extremely difficult to get it from a diet alone, even a healthy one, as the best source of Vitamin D is definitely moderate Sun exposure, but also people who wear a lot of clothing that prevents the sun from hitting bare skin, also people who have darker skin will have a harder time absorbing Vitamin D as the darker the Pigmentation of the skin, the more difficult it is for the skin to effectively absorb Vitamin D. Would you believe that even wearing some sunscreens can block Vitamin D absorption, so don't go crazy with it despite it being important in protecting us from UV rays. Although the government recommends that everyone take a 400 IU Vitamin D supplement daily due to the government estimating that around 25 per cent of teenagers and adults in the UK alone having low levels of vitamin D, which puts them at risk of developing longer term health detriments, like as we discovered Osteoporosis. There are several ways that you can take Vitamin D in order to ensure you avoid deficiency, you could decide to take 400 IU to 1000 IU on a daily, or you could even take 4000 IU a few times a week, the reason that you may want to consider taking 4000 IU a few times a week is that taking a higher dosage of Vitamin D in one go less often tends to be better absorbed by the body compared to taking a lower dosage more often (Especially if your deficient in Magnesium, which we will get onto later in the Magnesium section) It is especially important for over 60 to take a Vitamin D supplement, because unfortunately as we age, our bodies become less and less effective in making and absorbing Vitamin D. So, if you do decide to take my advice on board and take a Vitamin D supplement the upper limit is 4000IU, in other words I would only ever suggest taking this amount of Vitamin D, if you had been diagnosed with a severe deficiency and suggested to take this strength by a qualified Doctor.

Taking a Vitamin D supplement should also be considered by those who are pregnant, not only will this keep the immunity of the mother topped up (especially in the Winter months) but it will also ensure that the baby will also have a healthy development as a growing baby in the womb cannot produce its own Vitamin D, so it's essential that the mother is able to provide the baby with adequate amounts of Vitamin D to ensure full development, but also to keep the baby HAPPY!

Potential Risks

Now although Vitamin D is vital to our overall health, due to Vitamin D being a Fat-Soluble Vitamin (meaning that it is stored in the Liver) the potential of overdosing can be a potential danger. Too much Vitamin D in the blood overtime can lead to a condition called Hypercalcemia, which can cause the bones to weaken, cause constipation and diahorrea, create nasty kidney stones and even interfere with the electrical impulses that regulate the heartbeat, causing the heart to beat irregularly. However, as long as you stick to government guidelines, you will be just fine.

To find Vitamin D naturally in foods is very rare and they can be difficult to source compared to the other Vitamins (especially Vitamin B). Most of our Vitamin D needs come from direct sunlight and the good thing is that we don't need to be out in the Sun for hours, even twenty minutes should be enough (be cautious using sun creams as some can affect how well our bodies absorb Vitamin D from the Sun though)

Food Sources

If you're getting grumpy because I haven't told you any food sources of Vitamin D yet then here you are, Cod Liver oil (yuck) Mushrooms (That's better) Eggs, cheese. Milk (Calcium and Vitamin D in one) and yogurt, but also fortified breakfast cereals found in your everyday supermarkets. To be honest though it's going to be tricky to truly find good levels of Vitamin D from foods, compared to other Vitamins, especially the B Vitamins, so without a doubt its best to get our Vitamin D from safe sun exposure or supplementation, even twenty minutes of sun exposure should be enough, but don't go crazy as I'm sure that you know that too much Sun exposure can cause premature skin aging and even the mutation of genes which can lead to an increased risk in developing skin cancer in more serious cases.

Summary

- Vitamin D supports the overall strength and Density of bones, by helping to absorb Calcium effectively into the body.
- Vitamin D also helps preserve dental health due to its antioxidant effects which reduce the chances of developing gum disease
- If you're ever feeling a little blue? Not to worry as Vitamin D helps the body to convert Tryptophan into Melatonin, which is important in regulating mood.
- It is recommended that everyone should be taking a Vitamin D supplement, minimum of 400 IU, especially during the winter months where it will be much more difficult to get all our Vitamin D needs from the Sunshine.

Vitamin E (The Elderly Vitamin)

Ever wanted something that's going to protect you from the unwanted effects of aging, are you one of those people who is looking in the mirror and seeing an unwanted reflection of dull skin, marks, dryness, but worse of all WRINKLES! "OH NO! I'm sure I didn't have that wrinkle a week ago." Well let me stop you there, take a deep breath, and let's discover how Vitamin E has the potential of reversing the clock. (Just think Eternal youth). The main way that Vitamin E helps to slow down the effects of aging is because of its amazing antioxidant effects, the antioxidant effects that Vitamin E possesses help to fight against the damaging effects that free radicals can cause. In this instance increased signs of aging like inflammation wrinkles. Vitamin E can help you say goodbye to all of that, especially the wrinkles:) Before we dive a little deeper into the benefits of Vitamin E, it is worth noting that Vitamin E is a Fat-Soluble Vitamin meaning that it is stored in the Liver, meaning that it's *NOT* essential to get it every day through diet, unlike the Water-Soluble Vitamins, such as Vitamin C.

Now turning the clock back onto the anti-aging properties, Vitamin E also has the ability to restore and maintain healthy skin as we age because it can even be applied topically which means that Vitamin E can act as a powerful moisturiser, so yeah, it's really true that Vitamin E can slow and even reverse the clock. Vitamin E is also unique because compared to all the other Vitamins (except Vitamin A) it can be applied topically as a cream or an oil such as anti-aging creams, eye serums, sunscreens, or even makeup that can be found in many retailers and online, but guess what? Vitamin E can be also taken as a supplement as well making it very versatile indeed. Vitamin E is effective because it is easily absorbed into the skin, therefore topical use of Vitamin E may reduce the damage to the skin due to its antioxidant properties which help to protect us from the damaging UV rays from the Sun. Vitamin E could also help to keep our scalp healthy and prevent hair loss as we age, you should now be able to tell me why? Although there is no actual hard evidence to support this claim, yes would you believe it, it could be put down to the antioxidant effects of Vitamin E that reduce the oxidative stress in the scalp who may be linked to alopecia. Vitamin E when applied topically also helps to keep our skin moisturised helping to prevent dryness and keep our skin soft and elastic. The antioxidant abilities of Vitamin E can also help protect our eyes from damage, such as UV rays from the Sun. Vitamin E also helps to protect the inner vessels of our eyes such as the Retina, but I don't think it would be a good idea to rub Vitamin E cream over your eyes though. Anyway, moving on from discussing why it's probably best not to rub Vitamin E cream over your eyes, Vitamin E can also work well with

Lutein (Lutein is a Coronoid that helps to preserve eyesight) but Lutein is also an antioxidant that helps to protect the eyes from the damage that Free radicals can cause. Wow what an almighty antioxidant eh? Both really can help with reducing the chances of eye diseases, such as Cataracts which can be caused by Oxidative damage causing a formation of cloud around the front lenses of the eye. Is there anything that Vitamin E can't protect us from?

Have unwanted high blood pressure that's through the roof? Well let me take that worry off you, as Vitamin E can help with that too.

Vitamin E has the potential to help those with high blood pressure by helping to lower it to safe levels. This is because of the antioxidant properties of Vitamin E, due it its antioxidant properties, Vitamin E protects cell membranes, nerves and helping to support the circulator cholesterol molecules from oxidation damage. The antioxidant effects of Vitamin E also have the potential of helping to dilute blood vessels which then has the result of increasing blood flow around the body, therefore helping to lower blood pressure and putt less strain on our body. (Does that help you feel less pressured?

Potential Risks

Natural Vitamin E from diet, has been associated with very few side effects, if any. However, taking excessive amounts of Vitamin E as a supplement can cause slightly more serious side effects, such as increasing the risk of

48

bleeding, especially if you are taking blood thinners such as Aspirin.

Unfortunately, it is also possible for other medications can interact with Vitamin E, so always be sure to check your own medication interacts before considering taking a Vitamin E supplement as well.

Summary

- Vitamin E may help to slow aging by reducing the damage that free radicals put on the skin such as from pollution, this is due to the antioxidant effects of Vitamin E that helps to protect the skin from damage
- Another way that the antioxidant effects of Vitamin E come in handy is to support those with high blood pressure by dilating the blood vessels, and helping to improve blood flow around the body.

Food sources for Vitamin E include Peanuts, Hazelnuts, Macadamia nuts, Avocados (Nice!) and Brazil nuts

Vitamin K (The Cuts and Breaks Vitamin)

Are you one of those people who feels like it takes an eternity for a tiny and insignificant cut or wound to heal? Well not to worry as the magical healing powers of Vitamin K can soon help you heal in no time.

Before I tell you more about this magical mysterious Vitamin that stops wounds in their tracks, Vitamin K coms in two forms K1 and K2. Vitamin K1 is provided by plant foods, particularly green foods such as Kale (personally not a fan) spinach, broccoli, and Brussel sprouts. However, Vitamin K2 comes from a wider variety of foods such as pork, chicken, and cheese, but is also found in fermented foods such as yogurts. It has been shown that Vitamin K2 is overall better absorbed by the body due to its higher bioavailability because K2 typically comes from food sources that have natural Fat in them anyway, and this helps to increase absorption. Something to also point out is that having adequate amounts of friendly bacteria in our gut can also promote our intestines to make K2 as well.

Overall the main benefit from having healthy amounts of Vitamin K in your diet is to support healthy and quick healing from a wound, Vitamin K has the potential to help this by helping our bodies to form Collagen (the protein that makes up to makes up 90 per cent of the skin and keeps skin healthy and elastic) therefore the more collagen that is formed the more elastic and healthy our skin will be, resulting in the skin being able to heal itself quicker, now that's what I call super speed healing!

Vitamin K also has the potential of helping to support strong bones and allow our bones to have a healthy density, especially as we age, I'm sure you know that as we age, our bodies can start to declines, but that doesn't mean that we can't slow it down. This may be because vitamin K can help to activate osteocalcin (a protein which helps to form strong bones) which is important as it helps our bones draw calcium from our blood vessels and turn it into healthy bone tissue, without Vitamin K our body would simply be unable to make various Proteins that are important to our health. That is why Vitamin D and Vitamin K work well together and is also why you can find specific Vitamin D and K supplements, in which both are together. As sufficient levels of Vitamin D and K can really maximise our overall bone health. Vitamin K is therefore also important in the development of bone health in children allowing them to successfully peak to full strength. On the contrary, a lack of Vitamin K may lead to a child to grow up with weaker bones and an overall greater risk of fractures and breaks. In addition, Vitamin K can help reduce the chances of degenerative bone issues, most notably reducing the risk of Osteoporosis.

Another key function of Vitamin K is to also help with blood clotting, this is because Vitamin K is needed to activate several proteins that are critical for blood clotting, as a result Vitamin K has the potential to counter blood thinning medicines. So, if your deficient in Vitamin K you may find that you bruise easier and have frequent nosebleeds, which is another tell-tale sign that you could be deficient in Vitamin K. To be fair if you're eating plenty of greens, you'll be just fine. Although Vitamin K is technically a Fat-Soluble Vitamin, Vitamin K is unique because unlike the other Fat Soluble Vitamins (D and K) Vitamin K tends to be broken down very quickly and excreted in the Urine, so even if you go a bit mad on the Supplements, you'll most likely be safe, this as a result makes Vitamin K quite unique compared to the other Fat Soluble Vitamins such as Vitamin D.

Potential Risks

Overall, there is a lack of evidence to suggest that there are any serious side effects from Vitamin K. Deficiency in Vitamin K tends to be rare among adults, assuming that you have the right nutrition of course, but Vitamin K deficiency tends to be more common among infants. However, be careful if you're on any medication as it is known that some medications can decrease the levels of Vitamin K in the body (such as Warfarin) so always be sure to check that there are no interactions with a doctor or a Pharmacist, although the internet can be a great place to find information, I would take caution with what you read.

Summary

- Vitamin K works effectively with Vitamin D to support and maintain bone strength and density especially in growing children, but also reduce the risk of bone diseases such as osteoporosis, which only increases with age.

- Vitamin K has the potential of speeding up wound recovery, this is done by increasing Collagen production in the body which helps to support skin strength and elasticity (collagen makes up to 90 per cent of skin tissue but declines with age)

- Vitamin K helps to support the blood clotting process, as Vitamin K is crucial in activating several Proteins in the body that help with this process.

Well, my friend, can you believe it? We have just arrived at the halfway stop of our journey together; do you fancy a quick bite to eat? Drinks on me? Jokes I had better not, I'm the one driving.

I hope that you have enjoyed the ride in the passenger side (hope I haven't been driving too fast) but I also thank you for deciding to take this journey with me, I have really enjoyed it so far. Of course with your great company, I hope that the first part of our Discovery has been educational for you, thank you for trusting me with your valuable time, in the pursuit of a happier and healthier tomorrow. Anyway, let's carry on!

Minerals

Before we dive deeper into each specific mineral, I just want to give you a little bit of background knowledge to minerals, unlike Vitamins our body does not produce minerals, so it is even more essential that we get minerals from our diet. Minerals have many functions in the body (we will get to more specifics later) but minerals generally are needed to support healthy strong bones, muscles, tissues, blood pressure and organs.

Minerals are also split into two groups called Major minerals (Calcium, magnesium, phosphorus, potassium, sodium) that we need to consume every day in order to stay healthy and also trace minerals (Chromium, copper, Iodine, Iron, selenium, Zinc) that are found in the body in smaller qualities (but still extremely important, especially Iron) Another name for classifying them can also be referred to as the Macro Minerals and the Micro Minerals.

So, shall we begin?

Calcium

I am certain that you will have heard about calcium many times in TV commercials and emphasising that Calcium is vital for the development of young children and even into late teen years.

Maintaining adequate Calcium levels is extremely important for everyone of all ages for different reasons. Calcium is needed for children and teenagers in order to allow their bones to develop properly and grow to their full potential, however, Calcium is also needed for adults in order to maintain bone strength and density as 99 per cent of the Calcium in our bodies is stored in the Skeleton and it doesn't help that bone density slowly starts to decline as we hit our mid-30s. Therefore Calcium is vital for maintaining a strong skeletal system, especially for women who are going through the Menopause, during which women become much more vulnerable to the risk of Osteoporosis. Due to Calcium helping to maintain bone density, Calcium reduces the risk of Osteoporosis (bone strength weakens and is vulnerable to fractures and breaks) hold on though because Calcium is just not important for our bones, our muscles can also benefit as well. This is because Calcium can also help our muscles to contract and relax by helping to send nerve impulses around the body, all further adding to the importance that Calcium plays in helping our bodies to move and groove. As we also learnt earlier in the Vitamin D section, having adequate amounts of Calcium can also support our dental health, this is because our Enamel is largely made up of Calcium, so consuming plenty of Calcium can help keep our teeth strong and healthy, helping to avoid gum disease or having to make that dreaded visit to the Dentist.

In order for Calcium to be effectively absorbed by the body, it is also vital to have adequate Vitamin D levels, as a deficiency in Vitamin D can affect how well our body absorbs Calcium. So be sure to stay topped up on Vitamin D.

One perhaps lesser-known fact about Calcium is that it may also help you fall asleep better, this is because Calcium (especially in milk) contains tryptophan, is it just me or does that sound like a great name for a Dinosaur? Anyway, Tryptophan is an Amino Acid which the body uses to produce melatonin, melatonin helps to induce and maintain sleep. This could therefore suggest that a deficiency in Calcium could lead to trouble getting to sleep, so make sure to have a glass of milk before bed, and in no time, you'll be Zzzz

Calcium may also help to keep your nails nice and strong, as Calcium is key in keeping the nails hard and preventing them from becoming brittle and weak. Calcium is also important in keeping the tissues in the nail bed strong and healthy (our nails are a good indicator of overall health) and Calcium helps in contributing to your overall health. So, another sign that you could be deficient in Calcium is brittle nails, so be sure to check your nails.

Potential Risks

Although it is rare to overdose on Calcium from diet, particularly if Vegan or during the menopause, it is possible to take excessive amounts of Calcium from supplements. Too much Calcium in the long term can lead to a condition called hypercalcaemia which causes excess Calcium to leech from the bones which weakens them and in serious cases can even be fatal, and so because of this I would be very careful if tempted to take high strength Calcium and Vitamin D Supplements together, unless you have been advised to do so by a doctor of course.

In other serious cases, excessive levels of Calcium may also cause dangers to the Heart, the excess Calcium instead of absorbing into the bones, is instead transported to the Arteries where it can severely weaken the Heart, and in the longer term could be Fatal.

Food Sources

Calcium can be found in many foods, but most notable sources include Cheese, yogurt, nuts, seeds and of course milk with a nice bowl of Muesli (Delicious).

Summary

- Calcium (like vitamin K) is crucial in the growth and maintenance of strong bones, especially in teenagers
- Due to Calcium containing tryptophan which then converts into melatonin, Calcium could help us to fall asleep faster and improve the overall quality of our sleep and can also help with anxiety reduction.
- Be careful though, as too much Calcium may cause a condition called hypercalcaemia which could cause calcium to leach out from the bones (yuck!)

Chromium

Struggling to lose weight and need a helping hand? Don't get too down as Chromium can come in handy.

Before we start, Chromium is a trace mineral meaning that unlike other minerals (such as Calcium and Iron) it is not necessary that we consume it every day, however, despite this our bodies unfortunately don't make Chromium so we must get it from diet (sorry to disappoint folks).

Chromium may have the benefit of helping with weight loss by helping to reduce sugar cravings. Chromium reduces our sugar cravings by regulating our blood glucose levels by supporting insulin levels. Optimum Insulin levels leads to reduced risk of diabetes but also helping to support the blood sugar of those who already have diabetes. Insulin is also responsible for releasing blood sugar into our cells to be used as energy, just remember to burn it off. It is possible that diabetics have lower chromium levels compared to non-diabetics but remember I'm saying its possible rather than certainty. Chromium can also help to prevent insulin resistance in the body, which is one contributing factor to Diabetes. Due to insulin helping to metabolise the body, this will allow the body to burn fat quicker, therefore leading to increased weight loss. So, another way that Chromium can help with weight loss is by essentially increasing our metabolism, helping us to burn off those excess Calories. Another key benefit of adequate levels of Chromium is that it may reduce the number of bad bacteria in the body, as our sugar cravings are reduced (high sugar foods to tend to stimulate bad bacteria in the body) hence decreasing the risk of illness (killing two birds with one stone benefit here!)

Potential Risks

Overall, there are no real major risks associated with Chromium, however, too much Chromium from supplementation could result in stomach upsets, low blood sugar and liver upset. Also, those who have blood sugar issues (diabetes) should also be cautious with Chromium supplementation and women who are pregnant (however getting chromium from natural food sources is ok).

Food Sources

Chromium deficiency tends to be quite rare as it is highly accessible in a high variety of foods such as Apples, Beef, Grape Juice, Green Beans and Orange Juice, but even if you are deficient in Chromium, you probably won't experience any negative effects due to Chromium being a trace mineral. You probably won't feel a thing! It still won't hurt to make sure that you're not deficient.

Summary

- Chromium is a trace mineral, meaning that it is not essential to consume Chromium every single day and you probably won't experience any serious side effects if you are deficient in it, although it can be found in a high variety of foods, so deficiency does tend to be rare
- Chromium can support weight loss by reducing sugar cravings (sugar cravings can be a large detriment to weight loss) by regulating our blood glucose levels
- Chromium can help to support insulin levels that can help metabolise the body, therefore helping to burn fat quicker, in no time you'll be hitting those weight loss goals.

Copper

Not sure if it surprises you or not, but yes we do in fact need a little bit of that bronze metal called Copper in our bodies, while Copper is a trace mineral meaning that we don't need huge amounts of it in our diet, we still do need to get adequate amounts of Copper, as it is not stored in the body very effectively. Copper still does bring helpful benefits to our health, perhaps more important for benefits for Women, which we will explore.

One key function of copper is its importance in supporting the transportation of Iron around the body because Iron is needed to support energy, combat anaemia, and make sure there is effective red blood cell transportation around the body. Copper can indirectly be attributed to support all of these benefits. A deficiency in copper can often lead to a deficiency in iron as iron can't be transported around the body as effectively without adequate amounts of copper. Even worse a deficiency in Iron can also lead to a deficiency in copper. Being deficient in copper can also result in the Red blood cells becoming overall weaker and the Oxygen that they provide us won't be effectively transported to all other important systems like our muscles, especially during exercise. A good example of this would be when you are about to win the London Marathon, you clearly see the finish line in sight, nearly there, it's the final push, it looks like that months of training and sacrifice is finally going pay off. But wait! Copper deficiency strikes, your muscles start to become worn, tired, sluggish, and tense. NO! You end up stumbling to the finish line in 3rd Place. God forbid that would happen, right? That's how important Copper is to helping support our muscle function. Very important indeed!

It's also possible that Copper can also support the growth and pigmentation of hair, this is partly due to copper again supporting the transportation of Iron, and because Iron supports the formation of red blood cells, Oxygen is able to reach our hair follicles. However, another way that Copper could help with slowing the greying of hair is by supporting the levels of melanin (a group of natural pigments found in living organisms) but Copper could also block the hormone called DHT (Dihydrotestosterone) which has been associated with contributing to hair loss and greying. Due to Copper blocking DHT this could therefore strengthen the hair follicles and make them thicker.

Are you also one of those people who is desperate for a tan during the hot summer months, but instead you are just met with nothing but Sun burn and then back to white skin again? Well, you could be in luck as Copper can increase the chances of getting that tan that you've always wanted, as it helps to support our skin pigmentation by supporting Melanin production in the body. Melanin is a natural pigment found in the skin in which the body increases its production naturally when the UV rays of the sun hit the skin and the body also increases the production of the Amino acid called Tyrosine, which is also an important factor in allowing the skin to darken from Sun exposure. Copper could also prevent the damage of free radicals due to its antioxidant properties, this could also support hair growth by limiting the amount of damage and stress that is put on the hair follicles from free radicals, such as pollution and chemicals. Also, if you are relaxing and enjoying your time out in the Sun but getting worried about sunburn, then don't be. This is because Copper can help our bodies tolerate those unwanted nasty UV rays that come from the sun, that in excess amounts can cause premature skin aging. You know what that means? Longer and safer Sun exposure, and you know what longer and safer Sun exposure means? More tanning and more Vitamin D. Now that's what I'm talking about!

Potential Risks

One key thing to watch out for is that both Copper and Zinc compete with one another in the body, so if we have too much Copper in our system (especially from supplementation) then this can decrease the amount of Zinc we have and lead to deficiency (Zinc has its own important benefits that we will discover later)

Due to copper being a metal, excess amounts can be dangerous causing metal poisoning which can result in symptoms such as Liver toxicity (hepatitis), leukemia, diabetes, heart failure. So, as you can see there can be some very serious side effects.

Food Sources

Despite being a trace mineral, copper still needs to be consumed in adequate amounts to avoid deficiency. Foods high in copper include Cashews, potato, peanut butter, dark chocolate, Avocado, and last but not least lovely delicious Tap water from Copper piping.

Summary

-   Copper is important in helping to support the transportation of Iron around the body, a deficiency in copper increases the risk of a deficiency in Iron.
-   Copper can also support the Pigmentation of the hair and slow the loss of hair, this is due to several reasons, one being that Copper blocks the production of DHT (hormone that can increase hair loss) and helping to support levels of Melanin (which helps to support the pigmentation of hair)
-   Copper is a trace mineral (but also a bronze metal) that we need in smaller amounts to support our overall health.

Iron

Wishing to be a little more like Tony Stark? Out of all of the essential minerals Iron is probably one of the most important minerals in contributing to our overall health (and it's even more essential as we do not naturally produce it, we must get it from diet). Iron deficiency is one of the most common world deficiencies (especially in women), however, the good news is that Iron deficiency is very fixable and you'll be feeling like Tony Stark in no time.

One of the most important functions of Iron is to make haemoglobin, which is a protein found in red blood cells that helps to effectively carry oxygen around the body, therefore helping to support our cardiovascular health (good for all the runners out there) this can result in overall better athletic performance for all types of exercise but more specifically aerobic exercise. Due to oxygen being transported around the body more effectively, this links into the other main benefit of Iron in helping to reduce tiredness and fatigue. One of the most common signs of being deficient in Iron is Anaemia which can cause severe brain fog and the inability to think quickly, not good when you need to make a split second decision, but also Anaemia can also cause a shortage of Red blood cells in the body which makes it much more difficult for the body to effectively transport Oxygen around the body, it's even estimated that a whopping 30 per cent of the world's population is deficient in Iron, making it one of the largest world deficiencies. Another incredible benefit that Iron brings to the table is that we learned earlier in the Copper section, Iron is important in delivering red blood cells to the hair follicles, so yeah, it's true that Iron can help support our hair growth as well (Absolutely unbelievable!)

Probably one of the most important facts that we need to Discover is that for women, having adequate amounts of Iron is much more important compared to men, generally unlike women, men won't need to take an Iron supplement unless they have been diagnosed with an Iron deficiency. For women who are pregnant, having adequate amounts of Iron can also come in extremely handy as well, to improve the chances of going through a healthy and successful pregnancy. During pregnancy the bodies demand for Iron increases by a whopping 3x (Wow!) therefore it's much more difficult for women to meet their daily Iron requirements, compared to men, and this increases during Pregnancy and the Menopause and so this is when supplementation tends to become quite popular for women in order to meet adequate Iron levels. Meeting the daily Iron requirements helps to reduce the chances of a miscarriage, but can also decrease the chances of the baby having cognitive impairment, you're.   Iron is also more important to women because monthly periods also contribute to high amounts of Iron loss in women (especially women who have heavier periods) so make sure to check your Iron levels if you're feeling a little worn out.

Iron can also help with improving cognitive brain function, how? You may ask. Well Iron does this by helping to increase blood flow to the brain, and also by helping to transfer Oxygenated blood to the Brain, because of yet another incredible benefit of Iron, you may have a reduced risk of developing brain diseases such as Alzheimer's.

Potential Risks

While Iron is an essential mineral and does have many important benefits, you can have too much of a good thing (generally men won't need Iron supplements) but for women taking excess amounts of Iron may cause some side effects, one notable caution of taking Iron supplements is that Iron can be quite rough for the stomach to digest, so can therefore cause some stomach issues such as irritability (that's why I would personally recommend taking Gentle Iron as a supplement as it won't be as harsh on the stomach) and in the longer term taking Iron can even cause severe liver issues. Also, too much Iron in the bloodstream can cause Toxicity in the body, this is because Iron is known as a pro oxidant which means that in too high levels Iron can even damage cells.

Another potential side effect of excessive Iron is constipation, this is because Iron can slow bowel movements, especially if you take Iron supplements on an empty stomach, remember to have FOOD before! The good news though is that Iron supplements exist that don't cause constipation, also referred to as Gentle Iron, which I'm sure that you can guess is gentler on the stomach, so I would also suggest that you take Gentle Iron, if you do decide to start taking Iron supplements.

One common problem with consuming excess Iron is that it can cause a condition called hemochromatosis which essentially leads to a build-up of Iron in the bodies organs, and this can overall increase the risk of arthritis, cancer and liver problems (Iron supplements tend to be quite tough on the digestive system, be sure to take Gentle Iron!) Perhaps one lesser known side effect of Iron is that it can actually decrease our immunity to those nasty germs and pathogens, this is because while despite taking Iron initially in safe amounts and increasing our immunity as the immune system does in fact use Iron to kill harmful bacteria, excess Iron on the other hand can actually trigger the growth of bad bacteria and viruses, so be careful as excessive Iron can ironically cause the reverse, especially as people with hemochromatosis (caused by too much Iron) are more vulnerable to illness.

Food Sources

Iron can naturally be found in a high variety of foods, but more particularly in meats, so it will be naturally harder for vegetarians and vegans to get adequate sources of Iron.

However, Iron can also be found in beans e.g., red kidney beans, nuts e.g. Brazil nuts and almonds and seeds e.g. Flaxseeds (great on cereals, it's what I have)

As a side note, there are several things that can decrease the effectiveness of Iron being absorbed into the body, most notably Caffeine (most commonly found in Coffee, very sorry Coffee lovers) this is because Tannic Acid which is found in beverages like Coffee, reduce how effectively Iron is absorbed into the body (so if you have to drink a caffeinated drink, always leave a couple of hours gap if taking an Iron supplement). Not only caffeinated drinks, but also antacids, which may be used by women who are pregnant to relieve heartburn can also reduce the absorption of Iron.

Don't worry though as it's not all doom and gloom when it comes to Iron, here's some good news to brighten your mood, Vitamin C has been shown to increase the effectiveness of Iron absorption into the body. This could be partly because of the antioxidant effects of Vitamin C, which help to keep the body in tip top shape and work on stopping those nasty harmful pathogens from blocking how effectively Iron is absorbed into the body.

Summary

- Iron is one of the most essential minerals that we need to get in our diet (or supplementation) to avoid Anaemia, Iron helps to prevent Anaemia by supporting the production of red blood cells which help to carry Oxygen around the body, for example to Vital Organs.

- Despite Iron generally being widely available in a variety of foods (especially meat), a deficiency in Iron is widespread with about 30 per cent of the world population being deficient in Iron.

- Having adequate amounts of Iron is more important for women, compared to men, as large amounts of Iron can be lost particularly during periods and the need for Iron can increase by x3 during pregnancy.

- Caffeinated drinks such as Coffee can decrease the effectiveness that Iron is absorbed by the body, this is because Caffeinated drinks contain Tannic Acid. On the other hand, Vitamin C can increase the absorption of Iron due to its antioxidant effects.

Iodine

Iodine, is an essential mineral needed to make Thyroid hormones, and these magical hormones are needed to make some magical processes such as cell growth (but don't worry not uncontrolled cell growth that causes cancer).

Let's begin by saying that Iodine is trace mineral meaning that while we don't need it essentially everyday (unlike Iron) Iodine still does still have some extremely important roles in the body.

Needing a little support with weight loss? Well just like Chromium, Iodine can come to the rescue like Superman. This is because due to Iodine playing a vital role in helping our bodies to make Thyroid glands, and Thyroid Glands are extremely important in keeping our metabolism happy and healthy (Happy Thyroid glands usually means a happy metabolism) this can therefore help prevent thyroid conditions such as an underactive Thyroid in which the glands do not produce enough hormones and therefore the metabolism is not fast enough (potentially leading to weight gain) or an overactive Thyroid in which too many hormones are produced and therefore the metabolism is too quick (potentially leading to serious weight loss) but Iodine can help keep the Thyroid hormones that are being produced at a safe optimum level.

Like with Iron, Iodine is also important especially for women who are pregnant or breastfeeding. This is because Iodine is essential for a child's growth and development, a lack of Iodine could mean that the child grows up to have an overall lower ability to think and an overall lower IQ level, this is because the hormones that Iodine helps to support are vital for ensuring that the child has a healthy brain.

Potential Risks

It's very important to have just right levels of Iodine. If we have too much, then over the longer term, this can affect how effectively our Thyroid glands work, and of course how happy they are. Thyroid gland inflammation may occur which could cause serious Thyroid gland damage. On the other hand, if we have too little Iodine then our bodies will be unable to make enough Thyroid hormones, this has the unwanted side effect of the thyroid needing to work harder to supply these hormones with blood, this can then cause damage and strain to the Thyroid glands. We don't want our Thyroid Glands to be exhausted, do we?

Food Sources

Iodine is naturally found in soil, but of course you can't eat soil unless you would like to get ill, so better food sources for humans include dairy products such as Milk and cheese, Seafood such as Salmon, Scampi and Tuna and vegetables (remember your five a day) So certainly a good variety out there.

Summary

- Iodine is similar to Chromium in the way that it could help to promote weight loss as Iodine is essential in keeping up Thyroid glands healthy and your Thyroid glands are important, in helping to regulate your metabolism.
- Iodine is important for women who are pregnant or breastfeeding because of its importance in the development and growth of children. Lower Iodine levels could potentially reduce the IQ level of a developing child, so be sure to consume plenty if your pregnant as Iodine is important for your child's brain health
- It's important to not have too much or too little Iodine as either way it can cause damage to our Thyroid glands
- Iodine can be found a wide variety of foods such as Dairy products, sea food and vegetables.

Manganese

Manganese (sounds a bit like Magnesium, but I promise they are two different minerals, I like to think of Manganese as being magnesium's cousin) and it is important for several different functions in the body, but due to it being a trace mineral it's not essential to get it from everyday diet.

Firstly, manganese is important for our bone strength and density, by working with Calcium (yeah, they do like spending time with one another) but this is particularly important for adults over thirty-five when bone strength and density begin to decline decade after decade, therefore manganese (like calcium) could help to prevent osteoporosis in later life (but it could be argued that Vitamin D is more important). Manganese may also help support our Collagen levels (remember that magical Protein that keeps our skin young and beautiful) this is down to Manganese being found in the Enzyme called Proline, and this Enzyme is a pro at supporting our collagen production, and as a result potentially allowing quicker healing from wounds, which is one of the key components of Collagen.

Also suffering from those annoying old age aches and pains that just won't go away, well don't look any further as Manganese could also help with that too. This is because Manganese has some mighty antioxidant effects which can help prevent damage from free radicals that can cause inflammation to our joints and muscles, Manganese can therefore reduce degenerative diseases such as Osteoarthritis, particularly as we age.

Another potential benefit of having adequate levels of Manganese is that you may be better able to control your blood sugar and insulin levels, this is because Manganese is heavily concentrated in the Pancreas, and due to its antioxidant effects, there is the possibility that adequate levels of manganese could offer a protective effect of the Pancreas from free radical damage. Think of Manganese having magnificent benefits on the Pancreas.

Potential Risks

It is impossible to consume too much Manganese from just diet alone, so no need to worry there, the body will just take what it needs then excrete the rest out, it's all very clever. However, on the other hand supplementing Manganese may cause some side effects such as potentially raising Cholesterol and in more serious cases may lead to Magnetism (which is Toxic levels of manganese) which could lead to neuron conditions such as Parkinson's so be careful, especially to those who may have an Iron deficiency may absorb Manganese more (I'm looking at you ladies).

Food Sources

This super mineral can be found in several different food sources including nuts, seeds, wholegrains, and a big juicy pineapple, oh wait there's more, strawberries (perfect while watching Wimbledon) and blueberries (talking about this is now making me quite peckish)

Magnesium

I like to think of Magnesium as the older and perhaps the more mature cousin of Manganese. Magnesium is certainly one of the most important minerals that we need daily in our Diet for us to feel like we are truly rocking life, after all it is responsible for over 300 chemical reactions in the body, not only this but having good magnesium levels is also important in allowing us to benefit from the other minerals. Most notably this being Potassium, lower levels of Magnesium suggests that it can have a negative effect on our Potassium levels, so as you can already see Magnesium is one of the most important minerals that we need. What's even more concerning is that Magnesium deficiency is extremely common worldwide, it's even estimated that most of Britain have low levels of Magnesium (WHAT! Say that again) well unfortunately my friend this shocking stat is true, but don't panic as you're going to find out the importance of Magnesium, but also where you can get it from so you can fix that deficiency.

So, let's get started shall we?

What if I told you that Magnesium is crucial in helping something that make up a whopping 40 per cent of our body mass. Could you have an educated guess what it is? If you guessed Muscles then very well done, one of the most important key roles of Magnesium is crucial to help our muscles receive signal impulses from our nerves, helping our muscles to function more effectively preventing those annoying cramps and spasms. Magnesium can also be used as sprays and can even come in the form of Bath Salts (you can't beat a good relaxing soak in a bubbly bath), Magnesium, particularly when used in a bath salt form can also help to prevent cramping by helping to relax our muscles, (Potassium, sodium, magnesium chloride) are extremely important in helping to support the carrying of electrical impulses around the body, therefore helping to keep our bodies hydrated which is important in helping our bodies to keep on performing at a high intensity for longer (It is known that on the contrary that Dehydration causes severe Electrolyte imbalance leading to fatigue) Magnesium is also extremely important for helping our muscles to be relaxed, especially during the movement of contraction and relaxation, this is because Magnesium can help lower cortisol levels and also improve the Oxygen that is provided to the muscle tissues (particularly after exercise) so say goodbye to painfully sore muscles after intense anaerobic exercise such as Sprinting. It's not just our muscles that can benefit from Magnesium, our digestive system can also benefit from a bit of Magnesium too. This is because the relaxant effects of Magnesium can also help to relax our digestive muscles and the gastronemila tract, allowing our digestive system to run more smoothly and help to ease ailments such as Constipation, remember what I said about taking Iron supplements? Magnesium could really help with that. So, if you just can't get "you know what" out of your system, you know what the deficiency amigo could be. Just think of Magnesium as essentially an all-body relaxant, in no time you'll be as cool as a cucumber.

Magnesium can also support our overall bone health by utilising the absorption of Vitamin D (think of Vitamin D and Magnesium as BFFs) without adequate levels of Magnesium (which is very common unfortunately) our Vitamin D, especially when taken as a supplement remains inactivated and essentially useless to the body, and of course you now know what a lack of Vitamin D does to our bodies don't you? Yeah, that's right the chances of developing Osteoporosis increases and also a lower mood. However, Magnesium thankfully comes in handy so this doesn't happen, but on the contrary Magnesium can also help to bring down excessive Vitamin D levels as well, so it appears that good levels of Magnesium make it very hard to be deficient in Vitamin D but also protects us from excessive levels as well.

Wait! Are there any other cooler funky benefits to Magnesium? Yes, for your information there certainly are!

Magnesium can also help those who are suffering with high blood pressure which is an absolute big positive to take away from this magical mineral, I'm sure we all know that high blood pressure is very bad for us indeed as more and more strain is put on our heart to pump blood around the body, which can increase the risk of a heart attack or stroke. So, if you're worried that you have or could have high blood pressure, not to worry as magical magnesium is here to save the day. This is because of the relaxing powers Magnesium possesses can help to relax those tight blood vessels and reduce tension helping the blood to flow around the body, putting less strain on our heart. Yes, Magnesium really is a good all-round relaxer (All I'm feeling is peace and tranquillity at the moment – are you?)

Are there any lady readers currently going through the Menopause? Well would you believe it, magical Magnesium can help with that too. I bet you're now thinking is there anything that Magnesium can't do, after all Magnesium is involved in over 300 chemical reactions in the body. I know with important ones such as low mood, anxiety, reduced sleep quality and finally stress. One of the ways that Magnesium can help to support the symptoms of PMS is by lowering Cortisol, you should now know what Cortisol is? Can you remember?

Yes! Cortisol is the hormone that regulates stress, particularly during fight or flight situations. Magnesium helps to control the levels of Cortisol that our bodies produce and can therefore help to reduce the stressful situations everyone sometimes finds themselves in and it helps you to feel in a better state of tranquillity (you'll be sleeping like a baby in no time). The regulation of Cortisol is especially important for ladies who are experiencing PMS, because Cortisol naturally tends to be higher during the menopause. Another way that the magical powers of

Magnesium can also help to lessen the symptom of PMS is by helping to regulate the female hormones oestrogen and progesterone which do decline naturally in women, but especially during the Menopause. So, when Menopause does hit, having adequate levels of magnesium will leave you better prepared, so it's even more essential for women who are peri menopausal to up their Magnesium levels as this Magical mineral does often drop during the Menopause, always better to be prepared than not prepared.

Feeling a little bit of a brain fog coming on? Well what sheer coincidence that Magnesium can also support our overall brain health

Now unfortunately for many smokers, it's especially vital for you to get Magnesium in your diet, not only is Magnesium quite hard to consume from diet anyway, but smoking (like with other minerals and Vitamins) reverses the brilliant benefits that Magnesium brings us. Most notably smoking can increase blood pressure, something that Magnesium works wonders to prevent (poor magnesium) but smoking can also reduce the effectiveness that Magnesium is absorbed by the body. So, if you are a smoker I would advise that you take a Magnesium supplement and the good thing is that you can take Magnesium in a variety of ways such as a spray or a powder if you don't want to take nasty horse size tablets (I wouldn't blame you)

Potential Risks

Generally overdosing on Magnesium appears to be quite rare since most of us do need more Magnesium (that sounds quite scary when phrased that way) even through supplementation for most people should also be safe from any unwanted side effects, as the body naturally clears excess Magnesium out just like it does with a Water Soluble Vitamin. If you are one of those people who know that's it's going to be your luck to potentially experience side effects, then be sure to watch out for effects such as feeling faint or flushes (but these are very rare).

Food Sources

While many of us are simply not getting enough Magnesium from our diet we can still get Magnesium from a variety of food sources, such as a wide variety of nuts (Brazil nuts, Almonds, Cashews, flaxseeds) Avocados (I love Avocado on toast) Fruit (Banana, dried prunes) but without a doubt my personal favourite being dark chocolate and dark chocolate has some mighty power packing antioxidant powers which is always a plus.

Summary

-    Magnesium is an extremely common worldwide deficiency with most Brits having low levels of this mineral. Let's try to make sure you're not one of them!

- Magnesium is crucial in supporting our muscles by helping our muscles relax and contract (particularly important during intense physical activity) but Magnesium also helps our muscles to receive nerve impulses

- Magnesium can help those with High blood pressure by helping to due reduce the tension of the blood vessels, letting our blood to flow round the body easier and putting less strain on the Heart.

- Magnesium can help the symptoms of PMS such as stress and anxiety by helping to regulate the stress hormone called cortisol.

Potassium

So, Potassium. I wonder what it could do. Believe it or not Potassium has very similar functions to Magnesium (it's almost like they are both copycats of one another:)

Let's begin by pointing out that like its close relative Magnesium, Potassium also happens to be an Electrolyte as well. After exploring a Magnesium, you should know what an Electrolyte is? Could you give me an answer?

I hope that you would say that Potassium must help with nerve signals throughout the body in order to aid muscle contraction and relaxation, but of course it helps the most important muscle of all, the Heart! If you said that then well done, you deserve a gold medal. Not getting enough Potassium could affect our body's ability to effectively generate nerve impulses, as nerve impulses are generated by Potassium Ions.

Of course, Potassium does have some unique benefits of its own. One of the key unique benefits of Potassium is that is helps to support fluid balance in the body. To get a little more scientific Potassium helps to support fluid balance because around 40 per cent of the water that we are made up of is stored inside our cells, but interestingly Potassium is the main Electrolyte that is present (what a responsibility) and therefore determines the amount of water inside these cells to help balance the amount of water that is outside of the cells. To put it more simply, Potassium is important in helping to balance the amount of water both inside and outside of our cells. If there is an imbalance, then we have a higher chance of becoming dehydrated, especially after intense exercise where we lose a high number of electrolytes through sweat, which in the longer term could affect the function of our Heart and Kidneys, particularly the Kidneys in which Kidney stones can be caused. Also the powerful electrolyte powers of Potassium (like my tongue twister, just making sure your still with me) can also help with Water retention (which can be a classic symptom during menopause) helping to reduce Sodium levels by helping the Kidneys excrete excess Sodium, but of course as we have just learned, electrolyte imbalance can lead to the Kidneys to function ineffectively and they become unable to remove Sodium from the body, which can build up in our bodies especially from eating excessive high saturated fat foods.

Potassium does copycat Magnesium in helping to reduce our blood pressure by helping to relax the walls of the blood vessels therefore putting less strain on our Heart. Potassium helps to reduce blood pressure in several different ways, of course one of them being due to Potassium being an Electrolyte (copying Magnesium), therefore helping to conduct nerve signals which helps our muscles to contract and relax, and this of course includes the Heart, this means that there is less strain overall put on your Heart. The power of Potassium is also able to help remove excess sodium from the body which can help to lower blood pressure, that's why a lot of salty processed fast food can raise blood pressure (and anxiety) due to high amounts of Sodium that is within the food. Just to make clear, I am not telling you to ditch fast food, but I'm just saying be aware of what you eat on a daily/weekly basis as if it mounts up it can have a big influence on how you think and feel.

Not only does the power of potassium help to control excessive Sodium levels, which in the longer term can lead to higher blood pressure, but potassium's powerful benefits are strong enough to even help to potentially prevent Osteoporosis. This is because Potassium helps to support Fluid balance in the body, which in turn can help to reduce the amount of Calcium that is lost in the Urine.

Potential Risks

Now you won't need to get your pickle in too much of a twist about overdosing on Potassium, as the body can remove any excess Potassium it doesn't need (especially Potassium that is consumed through diet) however, if you're on any medication, particularly medication for High blood pressure, it's always best to double check before considering taking Potassium supplements. Rare side effects to keep your eyes open for can include confusion, excessive cramping and constipation.

Food Sources

Well, shall we have a look where we can get Powerful potassium from, I want a big enthusiastic YES!

Potassium can be found your typical nuts and seeds, tomatoes (a powerful punch packing antioxidant as well) but also Potatoes, Avocados and especially Banana's (You cheeky little monkey:)

Summary

- Potassium in some ways has very similar functions to Magnesium, due Potassium also being an Electrolyte, Potassium is important in helping our muscles to contract and relax, therefore extending to helping the most important muscle contract and relax, can you tell me what it is? Yes! That's right the Heart.
- Potassium can help control our Blood pressure levels, as Potassium can help to regulate Sodium levels in the body (Too much Sodium increases blood pressure!) but also because Potassium is an Electrolyte it helps the blood vessels to relax, helping to blood flow easier, putting less strain on our Heart.
- Potassium is essential for Fluid Balance, this is because Potassium is helps to balance water inside and outside the cells, therefore helping to prevent Dehydration (typical symptom of Electrolyte imbalance)

- Potassium can also help the body hold onto Calcium by helping to reduce the amount of Calcium that is lost in the Urine.

Selenium

Sounds a bit like a posh word for Snail slime (yuck) but let me reassure you it's not. In fact, some cool benefits are brought to the party when Selenium is around, so let's start getting some disco grooves out! What do you say? Ready to dance?

Firstly, Selenium has one almighty punch when it comes to its *antioxidant abilities*, do you know what an Antioxidant protects against? The correct answer would-be free radicals, such as Pollution and smoking.

Before we continue can you tell me which other mineral has strong antioxidant abilities? Go on have a go? Want a clue? Psst, it sounds like a man!

The answer that I would be looking for would be *Manganese*, if you didn't get that right then please don't worry, taking a large positive step in learning all this certainly takes effort, I forget all the time.

However, for men, Selenium is also important in helping *to produce super sperm*. So, if you are trying to improve your overall fertility health, you know where to go. Selenium can help sperm cells to grow to a healthy size and shape, therefore it can help with increasing the probability of having a healthy conception. Also, the amazing antioxidant abilities of Selenium, can also help to *protect sperm from the damage of Free radicals*, helping increase the chances of having Grade A sperm (you can google that on the internet, seriously I'm not joking:)

A good sign in men that you might be *lacking in Selenium could be fertility issues*, but don't worry more general signs of deficiency include shedding hair, muscle weakness and a weak immune system

Another ability of super Selenium is that it can also help to *support the absorption of Vitamin E into the body,* and vice versa (What a double whammy!) this is because Selenium and Vitamin E both possesses some awesome ***antioxidant*** effects, limiting the damage that free radicals cause to us. Selenium due to its powerful Antioxidant effects can also help to fight inflammation in the body, which again is increased by the presence of those nasty free radicals in the body, all the while reducing the chances of cancers, heart disease and of course mental decline.

Selenium also has the superb ability to help with supporting the growth of our nails and hair. Here's another one to test your memory, could you tell me what is the name of the B Vitamin which also has this benefit? Hmm. Have a go?

Biotin? It certainly is. If you didn't get it right, not to worry, these questions are here to reinforce your knowledge, if you get it wrong that's a good thing as you'll know for next time.

Anyway, lets back to Selenium shall we? As I was saying, Selenium helps to support the growth and maintenance of our hair and nails. This is in part because of Selenium antioxidant effects, which for one will help to protect our nails and hair from stress and damage from external factors (can you give me two examples of free radicals?) but also the Thyroid glands will be better protected also from oxidative stress allowing them to function more effectively, and as a result of course helping our hair and nails to grow stronger and thicker (it's all coming together now) Another way that Selenium can also make your hair fit for a shampoo commercial is by helping to remove Dandruff from the scalp, partly because the antioxidant effects of Selenium help to fight inflammation of the scalp which causes dandruff. No need for anti-dandruff Shampoo here!

The good thing with Selenium, perhaps unlike with some of the other minerals, is that Selenium deficiency can be quite easily spotted, with common signs of deficiency including brittle and thinning hair, negative effects on the Thyroid (quick weight gain or quick weight loss) and a weak immune system.

Potential Risks

Now while getting adequate levels of Selenium is important, of course, as we all know we can get too much of a good thing, and selenium is no exception to this. Unfortunately, too much Selenium can cause poisoning, the posh word for this is called *Selenosis*.

As a result, we could experience symptoms such as a Metallic taste in the mouth but also fatigue and cramping.

Food Sources

One good thing about Selenium is that it can be found in a super wide range of foods, catering well to Vegetarians and Vegans as well. Good sources of Selenium include Brazil nuts, Tuna, Prawns, chicken, eggs but also vegan friendly sources include Spinach, oats, and baked beans.

Summary

- Selenium contains some incredible *antioxidant abilities* which can help to fight against the damage of free radicals.
- Selenium can also come in handy when supporting *Male Fertility* by helping to support sperm size and mobility.
- Selenium can *support the absorption of Vitamin E* into the body, what an *almighty double antioxidant punch*
- Selenium can *support hair and nail growth* by helping to protect the Thyroid gland from Oxidative stress, this will help the Thyroid glands to function more effectively.

Can you believe it! We are now getting towards the end of our journey together, we are on the last stretch of road before we hit our end destination, look can you see the sign? There! Only another 20 miles until we hit the palm trees and the beach. Getting excited? We have just about enough fuel to get us there so no need to Panic… Just yet

Zinc

Now given the fact that Zinc is the only Vitamin or Mineral that begins with a Z, makes it unique in its own regard, but of course of there is far more to Zinc than just this!

Firstly, Zinc is one of those essential minerals that everyone needs, but especially men, for several different reasons that we will get onto now. Firstly, it has been suggested that *low levels of Zinc* lead to *lower Testosterone levels* in men, but what's perhaps even more important is that our bodies can't make Zinc, so we must get it from diet!

Zinc can also help with our immunity, quick fire question, which Vitamin helps support our immunity?

Yes, Vitamin C would be the answer that I would be looking for, likewise with Vitamin C, Zinc can also help with the production of those wonderful White blood cells, band also helping to protect our bodies from Oxidative stress. We learnt exactly how this is done in the Vitamin C section, but just to jog your memory, the whole process is called Phagocytosis in which the White Blood cells either release antibodies in order to destroy the Pathogen, or the White blood cell can choose to ingest (Eat) the Pathogen, yep, the White blood cells do have the choice with how to deal with Pathogens, Incredible!

Zinc can also help with our hair health, big beauty benefits await you! To get a little more scientific for you, Zinc helps to support our hair health by being involved in Protein Synthesis, more specifically the *Protein Keratin,* that is one of the key components of hair strength.

In addition to this Zinc can also support the beauty of our face as well (Not just limited to our hair) but for Zinc to be beneficial for our faces, it would be preferable for Zinc to be topically applied on the face. Zinc helps our facial health by helping to supress the amount of Sebum that is produced onto the skin, basically preventing our skin from becoming too oily, without drying it out like the Sahara Desert. Zinc also helps to prevent acne Bacteria from developing on our face, which can be caused by external factors such as dirt and grime from the environment. In no time you're going to have beautifully fresh clean skin.

Zinc can also help to protect us from Oxidative stress, and as a result can help with a variety of vital functions, such as helping to quicken wound healing. Zinc also helps to quicken wound healing by helping to support Collagen Synthesis, helping to keep our skin elastic and one tough cookie to break by external factors.

Can you tell me which Vitamin helps with Collagen Synthesis in the body?

It's the Vitamin that comes from nice ripe juicy Oranges (I promise that it's not a trick question), if you still haven't gotten my hint, its good old juicy Vitamin C again!

Anyway my friend, Zinc as we learnt earlier (hopefully you remember) does help to protect us from oxidative stress, but this protection can also help inflammation that can be caused by free radicals, because of this it is possible that Zinc can even give our mental health a good boost as Free Radicals can increase the chances of depression as they can inhibit on how effectively our bodies produce Serotonin (The HAPPY hormone Yippee!). For your final little test could you give me two examples of Free radicals? Ah, I would hope that you would have said Pollution and Smoking.

#Top class student.

It's not just adults though that can benefit from Zinc, but also teenagers and children too! A lack of Zinc in a child's diet could potentially affect their growth, but also a lack of Zinc could also make them especially vulnerable to those nasty winter germs and infections, so to ensure your child becomes super charged against those pathogens, be sure to make sure that they are taking adequate levels of Zinc, either through diet or even a child's multivitamin which can usually come in the form of a flavoured gummy.

Potential Risks

Firstly, one of the main dangers of taking too Zinc is that it can negatively have an impact on our Copper Levels, as

I said earlier in the Copper section, both Zinc and Copper do both compete with one another in the body. So excess of one can deplete the other one in the body, so be sure to consume enough Copper, preferably through diet, but a supplement will also be satisfactory as well.

Hitting the Gym hard? Well, there's a chance that if you're hitting the red line, you're going to lose Zinc through your sweat, so if you're a high intensity athlete I would recommend considering taking a Zinc supplement just to top your levels back up.

Also, people who do take excessive levels Zinc through supplementation, can find that this results in flu like symptoms such as fever, headaches and excessive coughing.

Food Sources

Here we are, the last suggestion of where to find food sources for our last mineral. Are you getting emotional? I am!

Good sources for our last mineral are meat (especially red meat) shellfish, dark chocolate, nuts such as Cashews, vegetables especially Baked Potatoes (I love Tuna on mine) and also Eggs are a good source.

Summary

- Zinc could help with male fertility by increasing Testosterone levels but by also increasing Libido (Sex drive)

- Zinc can also help protect us from Oxidative stress therefore reducing the negative effects that Free Radicals can put on the body.

- Zinc can help support the health of our hair, this is due to Zincs importance in protein synthesis, but especially the protein Keratin which is vital for supporting hair strength.

- Zinc can also be applied topically on the face to help remove excess sebum, and as a result helping to prevent our faces from becoming too oily which is one of the major causes of Acne breakouts.

The Arrival

We have made it! YES! Can you believe it? Look there's a brilliant parking space with our name on it, just before the beach. (Pulls in, Neutral and pulls the handbrake up for the last time) Well what one heck of a journey we have had so far. Let's find a nice place to get the deck chairs out, so we can now Discover a little more, how about some Herbal Remedies? Are you now ready for the second half of our Discovery? I certainly am!

Several times throughout our Discovery I have mentioned a fancy protein called Collagen but only briefly explained about it. To tell you just a little bit more, Collagen is basically the most abundant Protein in the body (making up about 30 per cent of who we are) collagen is the miracle to youth by helping to keep our skin strong and elastic helping to prevent wrinkles. Not only this but Collagen also makes up our Teeth, Cartilage, bones, ligaments, cornea in the eye, blood vessels, helping the blood clot, hair, and nail strength. Yeah! I know this is a large list, think of Collagen as our bodies scaffolding, helping to keep us glued together. However, behind these Collagen miracles, there is unfortunately one very big catch, as we age, particularly after our earlier 20s Collagen production in our body starts to decline naturally meaning that we are more and more at risk of sagging skin, inflammation, hair loss, muscle weakness, arthritis and of course the biggest culprit of them all: WRINKLES! What doesn't help though is that external factors can also further decrease the amount of Collagen that is in our bodies such as Pollution, but especially smoking as the chemicals that are produced by smoking can quickly kill the Collagen that is in our bodies.

Not to worry though as there are ways to limit the loss of Collagen as we age, so there is hope after all. This can be having a healthier diet, or taking even better actually taking Collagen orally as a powder or tablet, but the powder is by far the best absorbed into the body as the Collagen is broken down into small molecules called Peptides that are then absorbed into the bloodstream and they make their way to the surface of the skin. (sounding good?). As a result this helps to stimulate more Collagen production, allowing our bodies to more effectively retain the Collagen that it already has, which becomes more and more important as we age. Taking Collagen Peptides could be particularly useful for women who are currently going through the menopause as this is when Collagen typically tends to decline rapidly in women. Of course, taking Collagen orally isn't the only way to help boost our levels though, as we learnt earlier Vitamin C in particular helps to boost Collagen levels, so of course Nutrition also plays a large part in how well our body can respond in Collagen production. So, remember to eat your greens. Although it is inevitable that we are going to lose Collagen as we age, there is no doubt that we can slow down Collagen loss as we age too.

Well, there we have it friend, ready to go and enjoy some sunshine on the beach, it will be sunset soon so we had better hurry up on this Discovery, we don't want to be here until midnight, it will be freezing by then!

Before we Discover some Herbal remedies, I just wanted to point out to you that with Herbal Remedies their benefits tend to be much more subjective rather than backed by science, unlike Vitamins and Minerals, Herbal remedies may work brilliantly for someone but then for someone else they may have absolutely no impact whatsoever. So, it is all down to the persons own opinion. However, it certainly won't hurt to try any if you want to, but what I would say is if you are on any medication to always check with a GP as there is less much certainty with them.

Now let's Discover a few of them, I'm sure a couple you'll find interesting.

Ashwagandha

I would say that this is the Herb that is probably becoming the most popular with more and more people giving it a go (Even I have tried it).

Ashwagandha has been a traditional herb that has been used for thousands of years (So it must be useful) and it comes under the category of an Adaptogen, meaning that Ashwagandha basically adapts to helping the person deal with moments of stress, due to its mix of different Vitamins and Minerals. One of the main ways that Ashwagandha helps our bodies to deal with stress is because it has been suggested that it may help the body to reduce levels of Cortisol. Do you remember what Cortisol is? That's right, it's the hormone that regulates stress, particularly during those "Fight and Flight situations". Because of this it has also been suggested that Ashwagandha can help with our energy levels because we will be less stressed, and furthermore because of the ability to reduce Cortisol, it has also been suggested that Ashwagandha can help those who are experiencing mental health issues such as high feelings of Anxiety and stress or even be experiencing some Physical issues. It has been suggested that Ashwagandha can reduce the inflammatory markers on the body and due to this the body will feel overall much more relaxed. Are you also struggling to get to sleep? Ashwagandha can also promote a deeper sleep, helping you to hopefully get a better nights rest. This is because of Ashwagandha's ability to reduce Cortisol, helping to relax your mind and body during the long work week, in no time you'll be looking forward to going to bed rather than dreading it.

Do you also want to boost your memory and cognitive skills? Perhaps for an exam? Well, Ashwagandha can also help with that too. Recent studies suggest that participants who took Ashwagandha experienced greater memory recall and achieved higher marks in recalling information during tests compared to the Placebo group, this again could be because of Ashwagandha's ability to help reduce Cortisol, helping the Brain to feel more relaxed, and when we're more relaxed it always seems that everything just fits into place perfectly.

Another benefit of Ashwagandha is if you're trying to rip out some serious gains at the gym Ashwagandha can help to increase our body's ability to consume Oxygen (V02 Max) which allows our bodies muscles to keep on exercising just that little bit longer, this will be especially useful during Aerobic Activity like Running. Because of our body's ability to consume oxygen more effectively, this will also lead to a healthier Heart and an overall healthier body as more Oxygenated blood will be transported all around the body.

Potential Risks

Now, of course like with Vitamins and Minerals, any Herbal Remedy is going to have a few potential risks, although the good news with Herbal Remedies is that their side effects tend to be more subjective, when compared to Vitamins and Minerals.

Overall, most people who take Ashwagandha should not experience any side effects, however some people have claimed in the past to have experienced feelings of Drowsiness and sleepiness (But this may because Ashwagandha generally makes people feel more mellow) and other people have claimed to have experienced some digestive and stomach upset from taking Ashwagandha.

I would also advise to anyone who is Pregnant or breastfeeding to see a qualified GP before considering taking Ashwagandha. Also, people taking Thyroid medication should be careful as it has been suggested that Ashwagandha might increase Thyroid hormone levels!

Summary

- Ashwagandha can help to reduce levels of stress and anxiety by helping to reduce the stress hormone called Cortisol.

- Ashwagandha can help to improve our overall sleep quality, again because of its ability to reduce Cortisol, which is often one of the reasons for reduced sleep quality.

- Ashwagandha can also give your Athletic performance a good boost, this is because Ashwagandha can help to improve the body's ability to maximise its Oxygen consumption, which is beneficial particularly to Aerobic exercise.

Devils Claw

Devils Claw gets its name from the plant that it comes from, which supposedly looks like a CLAW!

Are you starting to experience wear and tear in the joints, or Arthritic pain which is starting to get in the way of enjoying your daily life? Well, this is when it wouldn't be a bad idea to consider taking Devils Claw.

It has been suggested that Devils Claw can help to reduce inflammation because of the compounds that it contains, and these compounds are supposedly able to help reduce inflammatory markers in the body. This is done by moderately blocking the chemical pathways in which signals are sent to the brain which tell us that we are in pain and that something is wrong with us. So there is hope that you'll be able to move with a little less pain whether it may be Rheumatoid Arthritis or tendonitis post exercise recovery if you've been hitting it a little too hard at the Gym, or even Osteoarthritis in which the cartilage that cushions the bones begins to wear away, some studies that have been conducted even suggest that pain and swelling has been reduced by even half! WOW! Sounds like a Miracle to me.

Another lesser-known benefit of taking Devils Claw is that it may help to support weight loss, it has been suggested that Devils Claw may help with this because of its ability to potentially reduce appetite and therefore reducing calorie intake, however, the evidence for supporting this claim has overall been mixed so we can't say that Devils Claw helps with reducing appetite for definite.

Although it doesn't technically provide any physical benefit, Devils Claw is very versatile when it comes to how you can consume it. The most popular way to take Devils Claw is in the capsule form, but it can also be applied topically as a cream onto the affected area, this is particularly useful for muscular pain rather than Arthritic pain, Devils Claw can also be taken as a liquid. So, there are certainly several ways that you can take Devils Claw.

Potential Risks

Although overall most people won't experience side effects from taking Devils Claw, there are still undoubtedly some side effects that might be experienced. One of the biggest side effects is that Devils Claw can make the stomach more acidic, which in the longer term can cause inflammation to the lining of the stomach and even in more serious cases stomach ulcers! This would be particularly harmful for women who are pregnant, so if you think you may be or are pregnant then always check with a GP before taking Devils Claw. The biggest solution to solving the problems associated with Devils Claw would be to take Cats Claw, which comes from the same family and has all the same potential benefits, and Cats Claw tends to be much gentler on the stomach compared to Devils Claw. Some people may also experience symptoms such as Diarrhoea and headaches have also been reported.

Summary

- One of the biggest reasons that people take Devils Claw is because of its supposedly powerful inflammatory benefits, helping particularly with Arthritic pain by reducing inflammatory markers in the body, helping you to carry on with those activities that you love

- A lesser-known benefit of Devils Claw is that it may also help with weight loss, this is because Devils Claw may help to reduce our appetite by reducing the hormone that regulates appetite called Ghrelin

- The biggest side effect from Devils Claw is that it can make the stomach more acidic which in the longer term can damage the lining of the stomach, but don't worry as Cats Claw can be a good alternative.

Echinacea

Are you one of those people who just feels that all winter those horrible colds are just completely taking over and you never manage to completely clear them You have already tried upping your Vitamin C levels (which is a good thing) but you just need that little extra to help combat your cold. This is when Echinacea can help.

The biggest and probably most well-known benefit from taking Echinacea is its ability to help reduce the symptoms of the common cold. Although the reasons for this aren't exactly known, it could be put down to Echinacea's antioxidant properties that help to protect our bodies from external stress, in this case Pathogens and Free radicals that increase the chances of us becoming ill. However, one thing to note is that the studies of how effective Echinacea is have overall been mixed, again showing how subjective Herbal Remedies are.

Because of Echinacea's antioxidant abilities it is also possible that it can protect us from oxidative stress, especially our skin, as several, studies have also shown that Echinacea cream has improved skin hydration.

Potential Risks

Overall, most people shouldn't experience any side effects from Echinacea (making it one of the safest herbal remedies to take) however, to the very few people who may become ill from taking Echinacea, side effects that might be experienced include stomach upset and dizziness.

Furthermore, Echinacea would also not be suitable for anyone who is allergic to Daisies or any other flower that is in the Daisy family.

Summary

- The main benefit of Echinacea is its ability to potentially reduce the symptoms of the common cold, this has been put down due to its antioxidant properties that protect our bodies from the damage of free radicals and pathogens
- Because of its antioxidant properties Echinacea may help to protect our skin from oxidative stress, therefore it may slow down the speed of aging
- If you are allergic to Daisies or any other flower in the daisy family, it would be best to stay clear from taking Echinacea.

Evening Primrose Oil

Here we are at our last Herbal Remedy, and one that I think any ladies who are going through the Menopause will certainly be interested in.? Whether it's your Mum, wife, daughter or even yourself you don't want to miss out on this.

Firstly, as with Sage, Evening Primrose Oil has anecdotally been claimed to help to prevent excessive flushing in women. This is because Evening Primrose Oil contains some very important essential fatty acids, more specifically GLA (Omega 6) which is crucial in helping to regulate female specific hormones. In addition to this Evening Primrose Oil also contains some powerful antioxidants which can help to combat aging skin, which can be commonly seen during the menopause when collagen levels tend to decrease rapidly, it's also been suggested that Evening Primrose Oil can also help the skin retain moisture better helping to hide those unwanted fine lines and wrinkles. Are you experiencing changes with your hair, is it starting to fall out as your body changes during the menopause? Evening Primrose Oil could help with this! This is because Evening Primrose can help to nourish the scalp with the fatty acid called GLA which can help to strengthen the hair follicles in the scalp, which promisingly has been linked to thicker and stronger hair.

As we Discovered earlier, Evening Primrose Oil contains some antioxidant properties which can help to reduce inflammation in the body, which can be very beneficial for our Heart too, especially during heavy periods which can cause high amounts of inflammation in women. Can you think of anything better? I think I can. It would be an even better option to pair Evening Primrose Oil with Vitamin E for one almighty antioxidant punch. The even better news is that this combination can be commonly found in supplements.

Potential Risks

Overall, it has been concluded that Evening Primrose Oil is very safe to take, although I would say that the longer-term effects of taking it appear to be unknown now. Some side effects so far that have been reported include stomach upset and minor skin rashes, but like I said this tends to be quite rare, so you should be A-OK.

Summary

- The biggest use of Evening Primrose Oil is to help lessens the symptoms of the Menopause.
- Evening Primrose Oil may help to support the health of our skin by helping to stop excessive flushing

(like Sage) this could be because Evening Primrose Oil allows the skin to retain moisture better.

- Evening Primrose Oil contains something called GLA which can help to nourish our scalp and hair follicles.

Ginko Biloba

Are you still interested to know if there's anything else that can help with improving cognitive function? Well then perhaps Gingko Biloboa can help, especially if you are starting to find it difficult to concentrate.

Gingko has been used by people for centuries and is known for its numerous health benefits, however, most notably for supporting our brain health and reducing cognitive decline as we age, particularly helping to reduce the chances of dementia. One of the reasons that Ginko may help to protect our brilliant brain is because of its antioxidant effects, which as we learnt earlier will protect our brain cells and our neurotransmitters from free radical damage, which increases the chances of developing those unwanted degenerative diseases like Dementia.

Ginko may also been beneficial to our heart as well, helping to reduce the chances of coronary heart disease. This may be because Ginko can help to increase blood flow around the body, which helps the blood vessels to open and relax. Also because of this, our other organs will also benefit, particularly our muscles and lungs as they will be more nourished with oxygenated blood, therefore it has been suggested that Ginko may also boost athletic performance but without cheating with PEDS. This can be put down to more Oxygenated blood being carried to the muscles to allow them to function properly. However, another great benefit is because of Ginko potentially helping to increase blood flow, there is the possibility that Ginko can also increase blood flow to the brain, and again this has the effect of boosting our Brain health, which helps to fight those neurodegenerative diseases (It seems that Ginko can really protect our brain doesn't it?) Wait! There's something even better though! There's another crucial part of the body that can greatly benefit from increased blood flow. Our Eyes! It has often been shown by studies that increased blood flow around the body can also greatly benefit our eye health, as more oxygenated nutrients will be delivered to the eye, which as a result helps to preserve protect our eyes from unwanted degenerative diseases such as Glaucoma. Some studies have shown that participants who did take Ginko in a trial did see an improvement in vision, however, this was not seen across the whole board, so we can't know for sure whether these improvements were down to Gingko. So super eyes, super heart and super muscles, sounds brilliant to me.

Potential Risks

Overall, it has been concluded that Ginko is safe to take and that most people won't experience any side effects from it, however, of the few people who have been unfortunate enough to experience side effects, these have included headaches, stomach cramping, rashes, and dizziness.

It must be noted that Ginko may unfortunately interact with some forms of prescribed medication as well. This most notably being interactions with blood thinning medicines, antidepressants and also specifically Ibuprofen.

Summary

- The biggest use of Ginko is for its supposed ability to slow cognitive decline as we age, this has been put down to Ginko's antioxidant abilities that help to protect our brain cells from oxidative damage.

- It's also been suggested that Ginko may help to increase blood flow around the body which helps to give our muscles, heart, lungs, and eyes a good boost of nutrition

- However, a word of caution if you are on any prescription medication as Ginko can unfortunately interact with a variety of different medications including Antidepressants and blood thinners.

Ginseng

Struggling with your energy and overall vitality? Perhaps you've attempted to up your Vitamin B levels to give you more energy, perhaps you're a Vegan and are still struggling to consume adequate levels of Vitamin B from diet? Well in that case it might be time to give Ginseng a go, the magical Chinese herb that has been used for thousands of years.

Ginseng has historically been known to support energy levels hence the reason why more and more people are starting to use it daily. Studies show that the compounds that are within Ginseng promote the chemical reactions in the body that produce energy giving us that much needed boost when things begin to get a little tough. Even better though because Ginseng is an Adaptogen it will be able to adapt to our body's needs. Ginseng can also help with anxiety and feelings of low mood, this could perhaps be attributed to Ginseng helping increase to our Vitality. Ginseng can also help decrease anxiety levels because of it being an Adaptogen, meaning that like with Ashwagandha, Ginseng will may be able to reduce Cortisol levels in the body, helping us to feel more relaxed and you may start to feel more confident in yourself. So you can say goodbye to any phobias, for me it's Nyctophobia.

Another benefit that Ginseng can bring to the table is improved cognitive ability. This is because it has been suggested that the compounds within Ginseng may help to protect the brain from oxidative stress such as from Free radicals. This may also be the reason that Ginseng can help to reduce our anxiety as it's been studied that free radical damage can cause mental impairment and overall increased feelings of anxiety. Therefore, because of this Ginseng may help to decrease the chances of developing Dementia or Alzheimers.

Now, if you're going to shop for Ginseng supplements to take it's good to know that there are two types of Ginsengs; these are Korean and Siberian Ginseng. Korean Ginseng tends to have a much quicker effect on the body and very quickly you're going to feel the best that you've ever felt, however, the effects tend to be short lived. The effects of Siberian Ginseng tend to take much longer to kick in, but they do last longer, so it just all comes down to personal preference. I would say that Korean Ginseng would be better if you need that short quick boost of energy, but Siberian Ginseng would be better if you have a long day ahead of you.

Potential Risks

Unfortunately, unlike some of the other herbal remedies out there, having side effects from Ginseng does tend to be more common. The most common side effect from taking Ginseng is experiencing headaches, however, this could be put down to Ginseng increasing blood flow around the body, which doesn't exclude the brain. This leads me to another caution of taking Ginseng. I would highly suggest that anyone who has high blood pressure to always check with a GP or a Pharmacist before taking Ginseng as it may make it worse. Also, anyone taking any sort of prescription medication, especially for high blood pressure should always check with their GP just in case, to check for any interactions.

Studies also suggest that taking Ginseng in the longer term will also reduce its effectiveness, so it's always better to take it in cycles to maximise its effectiveness.

It is also worth noting that it is advisable not to take Ginseng if you are a big coffee fan, as the effects of caffeine may enhance the effects of Ginseng leading to the inability to relax and in more serious cases it may lead to greater levels of anxiety and irritability.

Summary

- Ginseng is best known for its ability to help the body cope with stress, such as helping to reduce Cortisol, however, its main use is to increase energy and vitality when you're feeling drained.
- Ginseng may help to improve our cognitive abilities as it may help to help protect our Brain from

Oxidative stress, this helps to reduce our risk of developing degenerative diseases such as dementia.

- Ginseng comes in two forms; Korean in which the effects are quick but short lived and Siberian in which the effects are slow but longer lived.

- Be careful if you have high blood pressure as Ginseng might be unsafe to take, be sure to always check with a GP or Pharmacist.

Green Tea

Fancy a cuppa? But a cuppa that can give you a good boost of energy, vitality and a good kick start to your metabolism. Well in this case I think that Green Tea might be a good option for you.

One of the biggest uses of Green Tea is to help if you're feeling a little sluggish, wait only in the afternoon! Well put the kettle on and get one of those Green Tea bags in the cup! It has been suggested that Green Tea can help with our energy levels because it contains Caffeine, which blocks the brains ability to produce adenosine, which is the hormone that makes you feel tired and the hormone that slowly increases during the day the second you wake up (that's why your tired late at night as adenosine has been increasing all day) However, because Green Tea also contains caffeine and other ingredients (which we will get onto) Green Tea can actually help to give our mood a real boost while helping to reduce our anxiety. This is because the Caffeine in Green Tea also helps to increase the amino acid Glutamine and the Hormone called Dopamine which helps our body and mind feel calmer by helping to reduce Cortisol, helping you to feel unstoppable in the face of adversity. Green Tea might also be useful to you Gym Lovers as well! This is because as we have just

Discovered, Green Tea can help to increase the production of the Amino Acid called Glutamine, however, studies that have been done suggest that Glutamine may help to boost athletic performance and it's also been suggested that Glutamine is also an important building block for muscle growth, so if next time you're getting a bit disappointed in your lack of gains, Green Tea might help fix that.

Wanting something that can also help with anti-aging? I think you should now know what I'm hinting at. Hmm yes, I am indeed hinting that Green Tea can help with slowing the aging process as well! This is because Green Tea contains a compound which is called ECGC which is a molecule that can help the body go into a state known as Hormesis in which the body is forced to fight against aging, therefore helping to slow it down. Not only this but Green Tea also contains other powerful antioxidants which can protect the body from bad stress, in this case the stress and damage that free radicals can cause.

Are you trying to lose a little weight but everything you have tried so far just doesn't seem to be making any difference? The calorie counting, taking exercise, but you just can't seem to lose as much weight as you want to? Worry no more, as Green Tea can help with that too! The main reason for this is because Green Tea can help to boost the Metabolism due to the presence of Caffeine within Green Tea that helps the body to burn Calories and fat at a faster rate. Furthermore, the antioxidants that Green Tea contains (like ECGC) are also useful in helping to boost the effects of the body's natural fat burning molecules, in which the bodies fat stores are used as energy instead, which is why Green Tea can help to boost your energy and vitality, wow it's all coming together now! Are you feeling the burn yet? The burn of success?

Potential Risks

Although Green Tea should be safe for most people to take, I would say that if you have high blood pressure or are on any prescribed medication for blood pressure then I would be vigilant and would always check with a GP or Pharmacist just to make sure that there are no interactions.

I would also avoid drinking Coffee if you're going to drink Green Tea instead, I would say drink one or the other, as drinking both will be double trouble and you will be hit with double the Caffeine Also, if you suffer with severe anxiety, it might also be best to stay away from Green Tea as it can potentially increase the symptoms of anxiety.

Summary

- Green Tea can slow tiredness and fatigue by preventing the brain from releasing the hormone Adenosine which is the hormone which makes us feel tired and sleepy.

-   Green Tea can help our body fight aging because of the compound it contains called ECGC that allows the body to go into a state known as Hormesis.

-   Green Tea can also potentially help with weight loss by helping to boost metabolism due to the presence of Caffeine.

Lions Mane

WOW! What an almighty ROAR Lions Mane has, and one that greatly benefits our brain health. If there was one single remedy that I would recommend helping most with your cognitive health, this would be the one. If you're interested, Lions Mane is one powerful little mushroom and gets its name from the fact that its exterior looks like the Mane of a Lion, how cool is that?

Although there has not been a great amount of research that has been done into Lions Mane, the evidence that we have so far suggests that it can really help to prevent cognitive decline as we age, some might even go as far to say that it can help to reduce the chances of developing Dementia and Alzheimer's. So far this looks very promising. Evidence suggests that Lions Mane could help to reduce cognitive decline because it may help to promote nerve growth and even repair and rejuvenate the damaged ones. This means that there will be new and stronger neuro pathways leading to the brain, and this is what leads to greater cognitive skills, memory, and overall a better protected brain against illnesses such as strokes.

This also leads to a healthier nervous system which will allow our entire body to function quicker and more effectively, including the brain being able to send nerve impulses and signals across the body quicker as well.

Another promising benefit of taking Lions Mane is that it can even help to lift our mood, especially if you're feeling a little anxious and on edge, therefore Lions Mane can be used as a good antidepressant as well. This may be because of Lions Manes ability to improve the function of the hippocampus, which is the region of the brain that is vital for processing our memories and regulating mood. Most cases of Dementia occur when the hippocampus begins to shrink, so because Lions Mane can help to prevent the Hippocampus from shrinking, therefore it has been suggested that Lions Mane may help to prevent Dementia.

Potential risks

Unfortunately, not enough research has been done into the long-term side effects of Lions Mane and the evidence to back it up appears to be quite limited now. However, some people have reported to have experienced headaches and even insomnia in more serious cases, but you must remember that with Herbal Remedies it is all subjective, it will be more likely that in decades to come there will be more research into Lions Mane. It's so far been suggested that any side effects that are experienced from taking Lions Mane will most likely be down to allergies.

Summary

- Evidence suggests that Lions Mane could help with growing new neuron pathways to the brain which lead to greater cognitive skills such as memory.

- Lions Mane could help to preserve the hippocampus which is vital in reducing the chances of developing Dementia as the Hippocampus is the region of the brain which regulates our ability to remember.

- Lions Mane can help to regulate our mood and reduce anxiety, again because of its ability to support the health of the hippocampus, which also is an important region in the brain that regulates chemicals such as Serotonin which are important for uplifting our mood.

Milk Thistle

Before we begin, I just want to clarify that Milk Thistle is not milk (unfortunately) but rather a prickly plant with purple flowers and white veins with its main compound also known as Silymarin.

Probably the biggest reason for people taking Milk Thistle is to help cleanse the liver, although we don't know for certain why, its most likely that Milk Thistle can help to reduce the amount of free radicals that can cause damage to the Liver, which is most seen when excessive alcohol is taken, and there is too little water to flush out the Liver. Milk Thistle can be taken to help prevent a wide range of different ailments such as alcoholic liver disease, non-alcoholic fatty liver disease and even hepatitis, which suggests that Milk Thistle might reduce liver inflammation by giving the liver that little extra help to flush out any toxins. So, once you take Milk Thistle your liver might thank you.

There is also some promising evidence that Milk Thistle can also protect us from illness, this has so far been put down to its active compound called Silymarin which has been known for its powerful anti-oxidant effects that can help protect the whole body from free radicals that can cause harm to the body such as premature aging, however, it's even been suggested that Milk Thistle can even help to regenerate already damaged cells that have been harmed by Free Radicals. It has also been suggested that the active compound Silymarin can also help to reduce inflammation in the body by reducing inflammatory markers. Want something even better? It has been also suggested that Milk Thistle may also help to reduce the chances of developing Dementia as we age. This is because studies that have been conducted so far suggests that the active compound Silymarin may possess strong antioxidant properties that can help to reduce the amount of those unwanted Amyloid plaques (Even the name doesn't sound nice) that are in brain, which have been associated in contributing to Dementia.

Potential risks

Overall, most people won't experience any side effects from taking Milk Thistle meaning again it is probably one of the safest Herbal Remedies that one can take However, rare side effects can typically include having feelings of itchiness, headaches, and diarrhoea. I would also suggest to anyone who is taking prescribed medication to also check with their GP or Pharmacist just to make sure that there are no unwanted interactions.

Summary

- Milk Thistle is used by most people to detoxify the Liver, as a result of drinking Alcohol. Milk Thistle may help with this because of its compound called Silymarin.

- Milk Thistle's active compound called Silymarin may have some strong antioxidant properties which may even help reduce the risk of Dementia by helping to limit the number of Amyloid plaques that build up in the brain.

- On the whole Milk Thistle should be very safe to take, although in rare instances some people have reported to having headaches and diarrhoea. So, doesn't sound too bad to me?

Sage

Hmm I wonder what Sage could help with. One word? MENOPAUSE! Yes, it's true, over the last few decades the popularity of Sage has increased in use to help lessen the symptoms of the Menopause.

Could you be one of those unlucky few women who one minute is fine temperature wise, but then the next minute your internal thermostat is cranked right up! Well thanks to the help of Sage you might be able to reduce this excessive sweating and fluctuation in temperature, because of sage's ability help to regulate the key female hormones Oestrogen and Progesterone.

However, whether you're going through the Menopause or not Sage can also be beneficial for the health of our skin because of its antioxidants that can help to protect the skin from damage from free radicals. Some studies also suggest that Sage also can potentially even kill some of the harmful bacteria that can cause additional damage to the skin and lead to further premature aging.

Sage can also be helpful in reducing our Cholesterol levels as well. So far it has been suggested that Sage can help to balance out the levels of good cholesterol (HDL) and bad cholesterol (LDL) and Sage can even help to lower the amount of fat tissue that is stored within the body! This may also benefit those of us trying to lose weight. All this can also help with symptoms associated with the Menopause!

Have you always wanted to have whiter teeth? Well, not to worry as Sage can also help to improve our oral health, giving you those beautifully white teeth that you have always wanted?

So far, it has been suggested that Sage can help with our Oral health because it may possess some antimicrobial properties which can help to kill the microbes that can cause damage to the inside of our mouths, even promoting dental plaque.

Potential Risks

To put it simply there have thankfully been no associated side effects with taking Sage, presuming that you take safe levels of it of course. However, its believed that if excessive amounts of Sage are taken then the neurotoxin in sage called Thujone can cause severe damage to the body. Remember though that this only occurs if Sage is taken in excessive levels. So, remember to stick to the daily recommended dose!

Summary

- Sage can help to lessen some of the unwanted symptoms of the menopause, particularly excessive sweating, and hot flushes by helping to keep hormones in check.

- Sage can be beneficial to our skin by helping to kill any harmful bacteria that might end up on the surface of the skin as well as blocking free radicals from sinking into the inner layers of the skin.

- Sage could help to lower Cholesterol levels by helping to balance out levels of good cholesterol (HDL) and bad cholesterol (LDL) in the body.

- Sage may support our Oral health by helping to kill any harmful bacteria in our mouth which can then turn into dental plaque.

Saffron

Although Saffron is a much lesser-known Herbal Remedy compared to others, especially its cousin Ashwagandha, the "Sunshine Spice" probably doesn't get as much credit as it deserves, but at this point of our Discovery I think it deserves a little bit of attention. Because why not?

I'm sure that you can guess by its nickname that Saffron can help to put a nice big juicy smile on your face, and that guess would be correct. Well Done! Hopefully in no time all the gloomy clouds will be burned away by a bright shining Sun. Ready to spice up your life. Imagine if you combined the "Sunshine Spice" with the "Sunshine Vitamin" WOW! What an unstoppable combination that would be!

It has been suggested that the compounds within Saffron that give it its strong colour contain some almighty powerful antioxidant properties that I'm sure you know by now help to protect us from the damage of free radicals that can cause several detriments to our health. (I know this might be getting very repetitive but we're nearly there I promise) In cases of great anxiety this magical spice can help bring you back down to Earth if you are feeling a little worn out! The antioxidant properties can also help to protect us from other health detriments such as cognitive decline, worsening eyesight and higher blood sugar levels. So, to sum it up Saffron is a very powerful all-round antioxidant that helps to protect both our body and mind from too much oxidative stress that too much exposure to free radicals can cause.

Saffron can also support the overall health of our skin as well as it has been suggested that Saffron can increase circulation (blood flow) around the body by helping to dilate (open) the blood vessels that carry the oxygenated blood around the body. This means we get more of the important nutrients to our skin which then prevents the pores becoming blocked, which leads to acne, blackheads, blemishes and spots!

If you happen to be going through the Menopause and are experiencing a worsening of your skin, mood swings, irritation, or fatigue. Well would you believe it Saffron can also help with that too by lessening the symptoms because of its antioxidant properties? YES! One reason that we haven't Discovered yet as to why it can help with these things is perhaps because Saffron is a cousin to Ashwagandha. This means that Saffron may act like an Adaptogen as well, helping the body to cope with stress better. So hopefully with the help of Saffron the Menopause won't feel as much of a minefield.

Potential Risks

Overall, Saffron seems to have virtually no side effects, especially when it is used in cooking. However, as a supplement if you are on any prescribed medication it is always best to check with a pharmacist or GP just to make sure that there are no interactions. It is also advisable for those who are pregnant to check with their GP and midwife before taking any supplements.

Summary

- The vibrant colours of this "Sunshine Spice" contain powerful antioxidant abilities that can protect us from the damage that Free Radicals can cause leading to higher levels of illness and anxiety.
- Saffron may also help to increase blood circulation around the body, meaning that more oxygenated blood and the nutrients that it contains are all transported to the surface of the skin, therefore Saffron could help to support our skin health
- It could be argued that Saffron might be an Adaptogen, meaning that it could help the body to cope with stress better, this may be particularly helpful for anyone who is going through the Menopause.

St John's Wort

I really hope that you would never feel like this, but if you've become so anxious daily that it's starting to affect your quality of life then St John's Wort could be a good choice of supplement for you. Whether it be stress from work, anxiety after a stressful experience (PTSD) or even if your just feel in slump that you can't shake off, St Johns may help to ease the anxiety and in turn help you to feel less on edge. Don't worry though this doesn't come at the expense of having warts all over your body, the name comes from the day on which St John's Wort was to be harvested by herbalists.

It's been suggested that St John's Wort can help to fight anxiety by boosting our mood and having a powerful effect on the Brain (Not a bad effect though) and this is because St John's Wort helps to increase the chemicals in the brain particularly Serotonin and Dopamine, which in higher levels can help boost our mood and fight off low mood and even depression. Unlike some other Herbal Remedies, there is quite good modern evidence to suggest that St John's Wort works compared to Placebos.

Good news for those going through the menopause. Again, this is because of the ability of St John's Wort to help reduce our anxiety and stress, which often increases during the menopause.

Another way that St John's Wort can benefit women who are going through the menopause is its ability to possibly restore hormone balance by helping to support the Thyroid Glands release of hormones. So, you can now hopefully help to say goodbye to a stressful menopause.

Potential Risks

One of the biggest reasons for taking St John's Wort compared to antidepressants is that any side effects do not appear to be as common, making it very attractive to people, especially because it does not have to be prescribed by a Doctor. If you are on any medication, then as always it would be best to check with your GP or pharmacist, as it is known that St John's Wort can interact with blood thinning medicines and medication for blood pressure.

Potentially the biggest side effect that may be experienced from taking St John's Wort is thinning of the skin, which in turn then makes the skin much more sensitive to sunlight, also called photosensitivity, so if you do decide to take St John's Wort, I'm afraid you might have to say goodbye to sunbathing while you're taking it or at least cover up. Other side effects that have also been reported include fatigue and dizziness just in case you experience any of them.

Summary

-   The main use of St John's Wort is to lessen the symptoms of anxiety, this is because St John's Wort may increase the chemicals in the brain known as Serotonin and Dopamine which are known to lift our mood and fight off stress and anxiety.

-   St John's Wort can help lessen the symptoms of women who are also going through the Menopause such as that of stress and anxiety, but by also helping to regulate the Thyroid Glands.

-   The biggest side effect that could be experienced from taking St John's Wort is photosensitivity.

Turmeric

Now, out of all the herbs, I think that this one is going to certainly spark a lot of interest. Why? You might ask. Well, what if I told you that Turmeric can help to fight inflammation in the body helping to fight conditions such as Arthritis which typically increases as we age. Are you feeling more intrigued to know more about another magical spice?

Turmeric can help to fight inflammation because of the bioactive compounds that it contains, most notably Curcumin which is known to be a very powerful antioxidant which plays a significant role in protecting our body from oxidative stress, which is one of the biggest reasons for the symptoms of aging like inflammation and Arthritis. It's also worth noting that the antioxidant effects of Turmeric are further enhanced when mixed with black pepper as black pepper significantly increases the effectiveness of Turmeric being absorbed by the body. One of the biggest benefits of Turmeric is that it can support several types of inflammation such as muscular pains, Rheumatoid Arthritis, however, its biggest use is to treat Osteoarthritis, and what's even better is that scientists suspect that Turmeric actually lessens the symptoms of Arthritis, making it a very popular remedy to take among the older folk. I would call Turmeric the spice that kills inflammation and because it's been used for thousands of years it must be A-OK.

It doesn't end there with Turmeric, there are still a number of benefits that we still need to Discover. Another well-known use of Turmeric is that it can help with our digestion, this again can also be put down to the anti-oxidant abilities that Curcumin possesses, which can help protect our digestive system from inflammation that can be triggered by diseases such as Colitis which can cause damage to the interior of the stomach and the stomach lining, which as a result can cause symptoms such as IBS, constipation and acid reflux. So, you can now at least say goodbye to those stomach cramps. Turmeric believe it or not is also very beneficial to the liver, again this can be put down to the anti-oxidant compounds within Curcumin that help to flush out the liver, helping to prevent both alcohol and other toxins that can cause longer term damage to the liver.

Finally, probably a lesser-known benefit that Turmeric can also provide is protection to our skin. I don't think that it would surprise you to say that it is again because of Turmeric antioxidant compounds. These compounds, like Curcumin, can help to protect the skin from external damage that causes free radicals to harm our skin which can be a cause of premature skin aging. These compounds that Turmeric possesses help to act as a blocker which can help to neutralise the free radicals, helping to prevent them from causing damage to healthy tissue and reducing Collagen levels on the surface of the skin.

Potential Risks

On the whole Turmeric is one of the safest Herbal Remedies to take as there is no set amount that causes toxicity, making it very accessible to a wide range of people. However, while side effects can include slightly orange skin, rashes, and headaches these side effects usually don't tend to be very serious and only usually occur when taking higher amounts of Turmeric. As always, if you are on any prescribed medication, it is always advisable to check with a GP or Pharmacist before taking, just in case, as we do not want there to be any interactions with other medications.

Summary

-    Turmeric is an Indian spice which has been used for thousands of years, mainly for its extremely powerful antioxidant abilities that help to fight inflammation.
-    The effects of Turmeric are much more enhanced and beneficial when it is mixed with Black Pepper
-    Turmeric is also beneficial for our digestive system, again because of its antioxidant abilities that help to protect our digestive system from damage and oxidative stress.

\-   Although side effects from taking Turmeric do tend to be extremely rare, the most common side effect is experiencing rashes or slightly yellowed skin.

Here we are, the last Herbal Remedy, then onto something perhaps a little unexpected? Let's see!

Valerian

Are you one of those people who's been struggling with getting to sleep or worse waking up and are having trouble getting back to sleep. Perhaps you woke because you needed to go to the toilet, or had a bad dream, and once you're up then that's you for the rest of the night. Well, our Discovery together might have led to a solution for that. After taking Valerian, you should have absolutely no trouble getting back to sleep.

Although it isn't 100 per cent known how exactly Valerian supports our sleep, so far, it has been suggested that Valerian helps to regulate the neurotransmitters in the brain that can help to contribute to the feelings of being tired and sedated. One of the key neurotransmitters that helps regulate our sleep is called GABA which is known by scientists for its sedative effects on the brain. Levels of this neurotransmitter are said to be increased when Valerian is taken as a supplement. It has also been suggested that taking Valerian may help to boost levels of the chemical Serotonin which is known to help support better sleep as well as improve our mood which helps us to feel more relaxed and at ease. It is not just how you have slept that Valerian can help with, but also it can help to ease feelings of mild anxiety and even depression. This is in part because of Valerian's ability to potentially help to increase the levels of Serotonin in the body, which has in turn been linked to higher moods in participants compared to those taking a Placebo. It has also been suggested that the compounds within Valerian that give it that lovely smell also possess powerful antidepressant abilities helping to take the edge off anxiety.

Potential Risks

Overall, Valerian is known to be safe for most people to take, however, because of Valerian's sedative effects it might make it dangerous to use machinery or drive if Valerian makes you particularly drowsy. Furthermore, Valerian might not be suitable for anyone who is pregnant, or already on anxiety and sleep medication or when taken with alcohol as this may enhance the sedative effects of Valerian.

Other side effects that have also been reported from taking Valerian include headaches, high amounts of fatigue and abdominal cramps. Don't worry though as these side effects do tend to be rare.

Summary

- Valerian's primary use is to help promote better sleep quality by helping to regulate the neurotransmitters that are in the brain that control tiredness such as GABA and the chemical called Serotonin.

-     Valerian's ability to increase the chemical known as Serotonin could also help to reduce our anxiety by giving us an uplifted mood.

-     The Sedative effects of Valerian might make it unsafe for those who are going to drive or work dangerous machinery! So be Careful!

OK then? And there we have it all the Herbal Remedies, what do you think of them?

As we are sitting here admiring the Horizon, something smells a bit fishy to me? I'm not 100 per cent certain what it is? Hmm I think it might have just reminded me that there could be health benefits of different fish oils, arguably more beneficial to women in particular as well. There are some fish Oils that can bring benefits to our brain and vision, while others can lessen the symptoms of the menopause. Now that is starting to sound interesting.

Are you ready for the final part of our Discovery?

Cod Liver Oil/Omega 3

Yes, this is the Cod that you can get from a nice chippy tea, the oil is extracted liver from the Cod, which is then formed into a supplement, Cod Liver tends to be a popular supplement to take because it contains essential Fat-Soluble Vitamins (We will get onto this) and some essential fatty acids.

Shall we firstly get onto the Vitamins of Cod Liver Oil? I think so! The two main Vitamins that Cod Liver Oil contains is Vitamin A and Vitamin D. The popularity for taking Cod Liver Oil comes from getting the Vitamin D content within it, as you should know by now that it is one of the largest world deficiencies that there is!

Therefore, Cod Liver Oil could be a good supplement to consider taking if you wanting to up both your Vitamin A and Vitamin D levels (just think two in one) especially as you know that Vitamin D primarily comes from the Sun which can be difficult to access in more Northern climates.

However, it's not just these Fat-Soluble Vitamins that Cod Liver Oil contains, but also some essential fishy fatty acids, how cool is that? These essential fatty acids are also known as EPA and DHA (you can find them listed on the back of Cod Liver supplements) and these essential fatty acids bring a host of benefits with them too! These benefits include improving vision, this is because large amounts of DHA are actually found in the Retina and is also contains anti-inflammatory properties which can protect our eyes from damage. Another important benefit that comes from these essential fatty acids is that they also help to preserve our brain health, this could be because of both EPA and DHA ability to help preserve and protect important regions in the brain such as in the Hippocampus which is responsible for memory retention.

I hope that you wouldn't be but, are you also suffering from general aches and pains. Research so far suggests that the fatty acids EPA and DHA can both help to reduce inflammation in the body, but especially DHA. So far it has been suggested that DHA in particular can help to reduce the inflammatory markers in the body, however, it's also been suggested that these fatty Acids can also help to reduce harmful bacteria and the free radicals that can increase inflammation. In other words these Fatty Acids may possess antioxidant effects as well, making it a good remedy for symptoms of Arthritis and Rheumatoid Arthritis.

More specifically looking now at Omega 3, there are also several beauty benefits that can come your way as well. Firstly, evidence so far suggests that your skin will be highly hydrated and better able to retain moisture better, which is extremely important as we age. Want something even more exciting? Well, I can give you that! Omega 3 can also support the strength of our nails and hair. Omega 3 can help to nourish underneath the nail bed by helping to lubricate and moisturise, therefore helping to prevent them from drying out and becoming rough. Are you also looking for an improvement to your hair and experiencing dryness or itchiness or you feel that it is looking Dull? Hmm yeah, I think that Omega 3 could help with that too. As with nails it has also been suggests that the fatty acids that are present within Omega 3 may help to nourish our scalp and help to moisturise the hair follicles that can become blocked, which leads to slower hair growth and duller looking flat hair.

Just a little side note to anyone who is Vegan and Vegetarian that conventional Omega 3 probably won't be suitable for you, however, the good news is that there is an alternative called Flaxseed which comes in a variety of forms such as a capsule, powder which can be sprinkled onto foods or even a liquid that can be drunk. The choice is yours.

Potential risks

If you strictly follow the daily recommended dose of taking Omega 3 as a supplement then side effects do tend to be rare, although it has been reported that some people have experienced stomach upset. However, complications potentially can start to develop more when taking Cod Liver Oil. This is because of the content of Vitamin A, which we Discovered earlier in the Vitamin section, where consuming too much Vitamin A over the longer term can cause a fatty liver and even Toxicity. This is particularly important for women who are pregnant as it is known that too much Vitamin A may cause harm to the unborn baby. So, I would say if you are pregnant or trying to conceive and are interested in taking Cod Liver Oil, then I would suggest going a see your GP for further guidance. I would also be careful if you have any blood clotting disorders or are on any blood thinning medication, as Omega 3 can affect blood pressure and the same goes for the Vegan version known as Flaxseed oil.

Summary

- Cod Liver Oil contains essential fatty Acids called EPA and DHA which can help to support our vision, brain health and the strength of our hair and nails.
- The essential fatty acid DHA can help to reduce inflammatory markers in the body helping to ease any aches and pains.

Anyone who is on blood thinning medication should always consult a GP first as there may be interactions which can cause severe illness.

Sea Buckthorn/Omega 7

Hmm, I'm guessing that you might be surprised to find out that there is such thing as Omega 7, and the good news is that there is! Fancy even better news? Well, I can give you some if you would like.

Drum roll....

Sea buckthorn is starting to be more widely used to help ease the symptoms of the menopause. And there you have it! Done

Just kidding let's Discover a little more about it, we've come this far.

As we have just Discovered, Sea Buckthorn can help to lessen the symptoms of the menopause, but how you may ask? Well one of the more scientific reasons for this is because during the menopause the female hormone Oestrogen tends to decline at a rapid rate, however, Sea Buckthorn can help to slow this down and even help to restore Oestrogen levels, which can help to keep those important hormones balanced.

Also, as we learnt earlier Omega 3 contains some very impressive anti-oxidant abilities and Sea buckthorn is no exception to this. With the anti-oxidants it contains Sea buckthorn may help to protect our bodies from cell damage, while the fatty acids that it contains allows our skin to become more flexible, this may be particularly helpful for women who are going through the menopause, when the skin tends to become much more susceptible to damage as it becomes less elastic and flexible due to Collagen loss.

Wanting something that can also help to improve your heart health? As we have just Discovered, Sea Buckthorn contains some amazing antioxidant powers that can help to protect our heart.

One of the antioxidants that Sea Buckthorn contains is called Quercetin, which is extremely beneficial to our heart, it helps to protect it from oxidative stress, therefore helping to further reduce the chances of heart disease! This is especially exciting considering that heart disease is responsible in 1 out of 4 deaths in the UK alone. By taking Sea Buckthorn it seems that you really can help your heart. Although it could be argued that its effects might be strongest on those who already have poorer heart health.

Potential risks

Unlike with the other fish oils, particularly with Cod Liver Oil, Sea Buckthorn tends to be much safer for people to take as it won't contain any Fat-Soluble Vitamins like A and D in which excess levels can cause Toxicity and a fatty liver. Although there has been limited research into whether there are any medication interactions, one potential medication to look out for is if you are on blood thinners as the limited research that we do have so far suggests that there could have interactions with Sea Buckthorn. Despite it also being unlikely for you to experience any serious side effects, it has been reported that lesser symptoms have included digestive upset!

Summary

- Sea Buckthorn can help lessen the symptoms of the menopause by helping to reduce the loss of the female hormone called Oestrogen.
- The fatty acids within Sea Buckthorn may help to keep skin moisturised and flexible, which can often be an area affected during the menopause.
- Sea Buckthorn contains the antioxidant known as Quercetin which can help protect our heart from oxidative stress, therefore reducing the chances of heart disease.

And there we have it! The end of our Discovery together! The full package, or what I hope you have enjoyed as a fully immersive experience. We have covered all the core basics that make up our health, what can potentially happen if we neglect one of these but also what we can try to do to improve it and help ourselves and our bodies in the longer term so we do not experience any detriments to our health.

I sincerely hope that you have found our road trip of Discovery to be as fun as I have. I hope that you will be able to leave this journey feeling that you have gained a little more general knowledge about the basics of vitamins and minerals and also feel you have a better ability to be able to make small steps towards better health. I really appreciate that you have accepted my invitation to take journey of Discovery with me. We have finally made it together and you have put up with all my enthusiasm about it every step of the way. I hope you have found it fascinating to learn a little about the Vitamins and Minerals that essentially make up who we are. Without a doubt they underpin our overall wellbeing without us even noticing.

Having a new found awareness will greatly benefit you in looking after your health for the rest of your life. Let's enjoy and live life to the fullest, but we can't do any of it if we don't have our health can we? And that is what this book is all about.

Wishing you all the very best.

PS. Remember to enjoy the sunset